Pink Flamingos
10 Siberian Interviews
Sonja Franeta

Dacha Books
2017

Russian edition by KOLONNA Publications, Tver Russia
© Sonja Franeta, 2004
© KOLONNA Publications, 2004
Copyright © 2017 Sonja Franeta
English translation by Sonja Franeta
ISBN: 978-0-9904928-4-9 (ebook)
ISBN 978-0-9904928-5-6 (print)
First Printed 2017
Second Edition 2025

Dacha Books
St. Petersburg, Fl.
Laredo, Spain
www.sfraneta.com

Dedication

For all those who spoke to me with such candor and care.

For the Moscow LGBT Archives members who helped me create this book in Russian.

With love, respect, and solidarity.

Preface to the English Edition

Translating **Pink Flamingos**, I fell in love with the people I interviewed all over again. What is significant about this book is that it captures the way lesbian, gay, bisexual, queer, and transgender people in Russia first spoke about their lives right after *perestroika*—in their own words. I recall moments in the interviews of inspiration and doubt, new thoughts bubbling up about experiences and new ways of saying things, startling even the interviewees. And the way friendships were made because of the intimacy of the process. A few feared repercussions or some kind of backlash in the future. I have changed names and cities to protect some at their request. I believe in the value of coming out, psychologically and politically, but I do understand the worries, too. The legacy of Stalinism and the KGB is hard for us outsiders to comprehend. Yet the interviewees' confidence grew through the interviews, an articulation of their identities and experiences, as did their appreciation for who they had become.

The interviews are stories in themselves. I would have asked my questions differently in the light of the growing consciousness around gender but the interviewees answers are informative nonetheless. There is much we can all relate to and learn. While the Russian accounts, in some ways, may have similarities to problems of queers all over the world, the unique history and politics of Soviet Russia have made an indelible mark on its citizens' lives to this day. Siberia, the land of prison camps and exile, is also a place where people have lived; it is a part of the broader Russian community.

The interviews were conducted during some of the most liberal times for LGBTs in Russian history, and they provide particular insight into Russian culture and LGBT problems today. Unfortunately, the Russian government led by Putin has been able to institute repressive laws that are aimed at suppressing the public expression of queer life. During the 2014 Sochi Olympics, Putin spoke about his anti-gay laws

1

as a way of "cleansing" Russia of homosexuality to increase its birthrate. The Russian Orthodox church is also very actively anti-gay, promoting negative views of LGBTs in Russia. Despite all this, people have not gone back into the closet. There has been a resurgence of activism and art supporting the rights of sexual minorities.

Two of the interviews, "Igor" and "Sergey," were translated by my colleague and friend Lara Ravitch. I translated all the other interviews. The interviews of Marina and of Katya and Masha grew into an essay in my later book, **My Pink Road to Russia: Tales of Amazons, Peasants and Queers** (2015). Marina died tragically in a fight near a lesbian club in Novosibirsk; she was only in her thirties. The final piece in **Pink Flamingos** consists of parts of Lena's and Asya's interviews and some of my story "Amazon Sisters on the Trans-Siberian Railroad," first published in the anthology **Lesbian Travels** (Lucy Jane Bledsoe, 1998) and included in my own book **My Pink Road to Russia**. Both Lena and Asya separately speak of their new love with images of flying and birds. Their interviews are fresh, youthful and full of hope.

One interview I did not include in **Pink Flamingos** was that of Kuzmich, a man who had spent 18 years in the gulag for being gay. When editorial decisions were made, I deferred to the judgement of my Moscow Archives friends who felt it would have been inappropriate to include. Kuzmich died two years after I interviewed him in Novosibirsk at the age of fifty-seven. The English translation and edited version of his interview is available in **My Pink Road to Russia**.

I thought about doing a "Pink Flamingos: Twenty-five Years Later" edition but was unable to contact all the interviewees to find out about their lives now, so the translation of **Pink Flamingos** is simply of the original version. All the other interviewees are alive and well, as far as I know. One of them now lives in the U.S.

A book presentation for the publication of the original Russian version of **Pink Flamingos** took place at the gay.ru headquarters in the center of Moscow in July of 2004. The room was packed and I appreciated the speakers' gracious acknowledgments of my activism and help with the Russian LGBT coming out movement. I loved looking out at the sea of friends and the many happy faces. **Pink Flamingos** was well advertised on the premier Russian site—gay.ru and featured in the queer bookstore Indigo in Moscow while it was open. An interview with me was published online with the odd title: "Sonja Franeta Who Loves the Word Lesbian." The lesbian journal **Ostrov** included a discussion of my book, as did people on other sites.

Here is one translated comment from the internet: "A wonderful book, very much needed by our community and not only by us! Now and for the future! Had I read this book in my youth, I could have avoided many difficult mistakes. Thank you to Sonja and to the publishers for your work!" (Olya)

The original video interviews, filmed by videographer Tracy Thompson, were shown with Anna Viola Hallberg's and Annica Karlsson Rixon's presentation of their interviews and photos in St. Petersburg, Russia in 2015 as "The Pink Flamingo Archives." The Moscow LGBT Archives holds copies of the video interviews as well. While these are only a small part of the interviews I did in the 1990s, I hope to make others available in the future.

I appreciate all those who participated in my interviews (whether they were in the book or not) and all those who helped this book come to fruition—the first of its kind in Russian. Thanks to the work of Moscow LGBT Archives members—Elena Gusyatinskaya, Victor Pismeny and Svetlana Barabanova—and its first publisher Dmitry Bochenkov, **Rozovye Flamingo** became a success and sold out quickly. The English edition cover was redone by Susan Zarate who based it on Bochenkov's 2004 cover. Now that it is available in English, it will soon be available in other languages and on the internet. I hope you enjoy this book.

Sonja Franeta

July 15, 2025 (2017)

Introduction to the Russian Edition

Why flamingos? Whence these beautiful and strange birds of all shades of pink, standing on one leg, going about their own unique lives? In 1996, I worked with several other organisers to host a queer Siberian film festival in Tomsk called **The Pink Flamingo Film Festival.** A year earlier in Tomsk I had met Sergey Kuzmin, leader of the sexual minority support group called Astarte. The interview I did with him is included in this volume. We talked about the idea of a film festival and then proceeded to organize it—he in Tomsk and I in San Francisco. While the festival was not a box office success at the October Theater in Tomsk, the reception in town was very good. There was much discussion and even support on the media and on the streets of Tomsk during the weeks of its presentation. I was featured on TV2 in a program called "Talk Show," where I spoke about the festival as well as my own sexual orientation. All week the festival was on the TV news; ordinary people were interviewed about their opinions and thoughts, and for the most part they were positive.

A few weeks later, a funny thing happened—a flock of flamingos mistakenly wandered into Tomsk. At the beginning of winter, they went north instead of south. Linking this misadventure with the festival, the Tomsk press joked good-naturedly about it. So I came to name my book after the Tomsk film festival and the poor lost flamingos who arrived after the festival ended and who did not feel quite at home in the Siberian climate.

As a member of the delegation to the festival, I represented San Francisco, an international gay mecca for gays, lesbians and other sexual minorities. On famous Castro Street, gays would cruise for a mate. The Castro Movie Theater, the store windows with queer paraphernalia, Cliff's Hardware with everything from rainbow flags to party decorations, and gay bars with loud disco music were all part of the open celebratory atmosphere of this very special area. It was the occasional heterosexual couple who looked unusual there. In the beginning of the 1980s, Castro Street was also a center of political struggle. Demonstrations for gay and lesbian rights were followed with demands for adequate healthcare for people with AIDS and HIV. Conservative forces in the U. S. showed their fierce opposition, but they could not block the progress to broaden the rights of same sex couples and families.

Many in Russia do not know that the U.S. has had a long history of gay and lesbian repression. It was especially severe in the first decade following World War II. The persecutions in the USSR were harsher with interrogations, coercion, and informants, and then locking people up in camps and psychiatric wards.

In 1933-34, the Stalin regime outlawed sodomy with Article 121. The punishment was imprisonment for up to five years. After that law was enacted, countless numbers of men were convicted and thrown into prison. Women were also harassed for their sexual orientation, though it was not explicitly forbidden by law. Women were charged with other offenses and relegated to psychiatric institutions. Article 121 was finally overturned in 1993 during Boris Yeltsin's term of office; however, this was not widely publicized. We still do not know how many tens of thousands of innocent people were put behind bars, harassed, or institutionalized, and still are, as a result of this law.

Because of the openings created by *perestroika*, the first Gay and Lesbian Symposium and Film Festival took place in St. Petersburg and Moscow in July of 1991. In addition to the North American delegation and local participants, six delegates from three distant cities—Novosibirsk, Barnaul, and Krasnoyarsk—arrived to take part in TV interviews and in demonstrations and actions against AIDS/HIV and to defend the rights of sexual minorities. Coming out of the closet would be the first energetic step they took in the fight against homophobia in Russian society. It was not until after the festival in

1991 that the Soviet Union would fall. It was still somewhat dangerous to be involved in an event like this.

After many questions from the Russian media about the reasons for her openness, Natasha from Krasnoyarsk said: "We did not come here to hide under a chair." Her friends from Siberia talked about possibly losing their jobs when they returned home. One woman worried that her mother would try to commit her to a psychiatric hospital. I was surprised at the courage of these young people and we quickly made friends. Of course, I also wanted others to become familiar with their lives.

We, in the North American delegation, brought materials and literature illuminating our experiences; we wanted to tell our new Russian friends about our personal life experiences in the "West." The 1991 Gay and Lesbian Symposium and Film Festival served as an arena where Russians and Americans could discuss their problems and issues. It was there that I started to interview people who impressed me and I wrote down their stories. When I returned home I decided I wanted to continue this process. I wanted to go through all of Russia and find people from every walk of life who were part of the so called "sexual minorities." That is how the idea for this book was born.

A few books and articles about sexual minorities in Russia had already been published in some countries; however, I wanted these people's lives to be explained in their own words. Since 1991 during my visits to Russia and further work there, I continued interviewing and talking about the rights and issues of gay, lesbian, and transgender people. I taught English in Moscow, and then I spent several years in Novosibirsk working on a project with people with disabilities, funded by the U.S. government.

In 1995, I had the opportunity to work with Douglas Conrad and Tracy Thompson on an independent film project focused on video interviews in three cities in Central Siberia (Tomsk, Krasnoyarsk, Novosibirsk). From 1992 to 1996 I was able to record more than fifty stories, both audio and video. The best were those recorded by videographer Tracy Thompson in 1995 and are the basis of this book. Although the film was never made, all of the transcribed interviews appear in edited form in this book.

Pink Flamingos was published thanks to the professional help and affectionate support of the Moscow LGBT Archives, especially Elena Gusyatinskaya, Svetlana Barabanova, and Victor Pismenny. Financial support came from donors to MOSAIC, a U.S. women's organization of which I was a member and others. The interviews were transcribed in Russian. One piece, "Amazon Sisters on the Trans-Siberian Railroad," previously published in the book **Lesbian Travels** (Whereabouts Press, 1998) was translated into Russian by Margarita Meklina. Many friends have supported and encouraged me in this project over many years. I am forever grateful to all.

Above all, I appreciate and acknowledge those who consented to do these interviews with me—for their courage, their openness, and their hope for a better life. Gays and lesbians and queers are everywhere, and have always been. Those who are feared, threatened, mocked and punished need a voice. May this collection be a step in that direction. I dedicate **Pink Flamingos** to the interviewees and to all those who were not able to tell me about their private lives, in hopes that this book will inspire more stories and promote social acceptance and understanding.

Sonja Franeta

2004

Olga

Interviewed in 1992

Translated by Sonja Franeta

Olga was born in Novosibirsk in 1965. I first met her in 1991 at the St. Petersburg International Gay and Lesbian Symposium and Film Festival. Young and attractive with lively dark brown eyes, she said the symposium had changed her life. At that time she worked as a nurse practitioner (feldsher, in Russian) and lived with her mother and grandmother in Akademgorodok, a university town and suburb of Novosibirsk. She writes poetry.

Sonja: You feel being a lesbian means more than just sex. What is it for you?

Olga: Of course, it's more than sex. It's very difficult to explain. It is my persona. It is my worldview. It is how I live. It's through my sexual orientation that I view the world the way I do. Thinking and feeling—that is me. That is the way I was born. It's like the color of one's eyes, I'd say.

Sonja: When and how did you comprehend that you were a lesbian?

Olga: I always knew it. I just didn't want to believe it.

Sonja: Even when you were little?

Olga: Yes. When I was three or four I fell in love for the first time. I had kidney problems and my mother was always taking me to some sanatorium. We would go somewhere very far away. We rented a room in a private house. The owner of the place had a daughter and she would take me by the hand and lead me to the river. We'd walk around. It was so hot there. I looked up to her and then I fell in love. I wanted to stay with her forever! Then when we left I really missed her and longed for her. Ever since childhood, I have always liked women older than me—my mother's friends, our female relatives. I didn't pay much attention to my peers in kindergarten or school. I've always liked older women.

Sonja: What kind of experiences did you have in school?

Olga: In school, in about fourth grade, I fell in love with a girl. I loved her for a long time, maybe two or three years. But I had no sexual experience. I was very much afraid. I wanted to, but I was afraid.

Sonja: When did you have your first experience with a woman?

Olga: When I was nineteen, I guess. I had a girlfriend, we were classmates. She came to spend the night one time. We lay in bed next to each other and talked for a long time. I wanted more, but sex didn't actually happen. I was afraid and I didn't really know how to do it. There was something physical. We were together for about six months, but we didn't have any real sexual experience. Maybe we were shy or something. I don't know.

Sonja: Then when was your first sexual experience?

Olga: It depends on what you mean by sex.

Sonja: More than a kiss.

Olga: When did that happen for the first time? A year ago. Actually it didn't have such a great significance for me. It was a girlfriend named Olya. I was completely indifferent to her physically. She'd come over, but it was not what I wanted. All the same whether she was here or not, she was not who I needed or wanted. And she knew that very well.

Sonja: Are you a lesbian or bisexual?

Olga: I've considered myself a lesbian from birth. As long as I can remember I have only liked women. I always knew I couldn't love a man. But I was always afraid. Wouldn't I want to have a family with a man like everyone else? Have his children, be with him always and go everywhere with him? But it seemed like a nightmare to me.

Sonja: What do you think about bisexuals?

Olga: What can I think? It's wonderful. It's the best thing imaginable.

Sonja: Do you think they are better than heterosexuals?

Olga: Yes, yes. They are the Golden Mean.

Sonja: Do you think there are more bisexuals than lesbians?

Olga: Yes, there are. But I can't say for sure, because people carefully hide that about themselves. It's easier for bisexuals to hide their sexual tendencies, than it is for us. It is harder for them to be noticed. Not every close girlfriend would confess this to you.

Sonja: Did you ever have a heterosexual relationship?

Olga: Many. When I turned twenty, I said to myself, "OK, that's enough. It's kind of silly to still be a virgin at this age." I thought if there was some real sex, it might interest me. But there was no pull towards men as it turned out. I went out with about fifteen different men, all kinds, good, bad, smart and foolish.

Sonja: What do you think of men?

Olga: Men are different beasts, not at all like us, a completely different species. Especially when you lie in bed with one. He cannot sense you, cannot understand what you need. He has only one thing in mind—to shove it in and pull it out. Then turn over and go to sleep. That's all. In the beginning, of course, he lies down, he crawls on his knees, begs and pleads. But if he gets somewhere, he becomes a barbarian. Every man behaves like a swine.

Sonja: Where do you meet other women?

Olga: Where do we find each other or where do we get to know each other?

Sonja: Where do you meet or find each other?

Olga: Nowhere. Sometimes we write each other and then we get together here at home or somewhere in town. But often I come across some pretty lowlife women. It's not really interesting to hang out with them so we quickly go our separate ways. I have a group of close friends. We get together at my house.

Sonja: Aren't there any meeting places for lesbians?

Olga: No, there's nowhere we can come and sit down and get to know one another. Going to a cafe would be very expensive. We can't even afford pastry and a cup of coffee.

Sonja: Do you have a place you can have intimate relations?

Olga: Yes, of course.

Sonja: Where?

Olga: It's not important where you have sex, what's important is to have it somewhere.

Sonja: Do you consider lesbian love to be perverted?

Olga: No.

Sonja: Do a lot of lesbians feel that it is?

Olga: As far as I know, no.

Sonja: Are there any SM relationships?

Olga: Between lesbians? There probably are but I haven't run across any.

Sonja: Do you ask your sexual partners what they want during sex?

Olga: I haven't had partners with whom I could talk about this.

Sonja: But do you talk to them openly about sex?

Olga: With heterosexuals? Or lesbians?

Sonja: With lesbians.

Olga: With lesbians, yes. I speak very openly about it. But, you know, we don't have any information about lesbian sex. We don't have our own books, or channels where they show films about us. Therefore, we really need to get together and talk. We get a lot out of sharing our experiences. We really need that exchange with one another. We often talk about these things.

Sonja: With close friends?

Olga: Yes, of course, close friends.

Sonja: Do you have any problems because you are a lesbian?

Olga: I only have one big problem all the time: when the feelings that come up for me are not returned by the woman I'm attracted to, when she doesn't understand my feelings. This always gives me pain. I haven't been able to understand this. I am always agonizing about it. I didn't think this was how it was supposed to be. Then I felt shame. I thought maybe I was perverted or sick. I worried that someone would find out and that's why I've been so lonely. I drown in my loneliness. I don't know what to do or who to share my thoughts with.

Sonja: Do you have a partner now?

Olga: No.

Sonja: Do you want to have a long term relationship or do you prefer to change partners often?

Olga: No, only long term relationships—monogamous and deep. I don't like the idea of changing partners.

Sonja: Do you want to have a family and how would you do that?

Olga: How would I do that? Well, first I'd have to find a partner and then we'd think about a family. I think it will all happen. At least I hope so. Later would come the decision about how?

Sonja: Do you want a child?

Olga: Not really, I just want a woman.

Sonja: Do you have any feelings of fear or loneliness?

Olga: Mostly loneliness, but I also have fears. The fear that someone I love would not accept me. And you can't do anything about that. Of course, it's so nice to see happy couples around me and that they are doing well but I am not in a position to solve my own problems.

Sonja: What do you think about the future?

Olga: I can't predict anything. I don't think about it. I have a very sad life, I guess, because I myself am that way. I get very tired of people. I often have to be alone to think about things. Sometimes the presence of others is such a burden that I lose all my strength, my ability to think, and I become like a limp rag.

Maybe I value my solitude too much and that is why I have problems. I am very picky about people, I am very demanding. I want to give too much. I don't want to have something with just anyone.

13

Maybe I myself am not that great. The fact that I am alone is probably mostly my own fault. I don't really know how to make it better. I probably couldn't live with one person monogamously, and see that person everyday, and be with that one person always. I'd have to have some breaks. I'd have to be left alone sometimes.

Sonja: In general, are you happy with your life?

Olga: I am happy and not happy. Some things are good, some bad.

Sonja: What is your work?

Olga: I am a *feldsher* [nurse practitioner, between a nurse and a doctor]

Sonja: Like a doctor. Do you like doing that?

Olga: At work I do feel like I am somebody. I feel that I am needed. I am useful in that I can save a person. And the work itself is interesting. One needs to think independently and quickly come to a decision, and also be responsible for one's actions. Of course there are all kinds of situations. We don't have good healthcare here. There are not enough people working, not enough medicine, and our vans are always breaking down. Sometimes you cannot give someone the most basic care because you don't have what you need. But all the same my work is very interesting.

Sonja: Do they know you are a lesbian at work?

Olga: Yes, they know. Now everyone knows. When I returned from the conference [the gay and lesbian symposium and film festival in Moscow in 1991], I told everyone. At first they were somewhat cautious. They asked questions like: "Is it true you don't want to be with a man?" "How do you have sex?" "Is it fulfilling enough?" "Is it normal?" I would answer—to each his own; some people like it. And they have all more or less calmed down. But a male friend who works with me, a very good friend said to me: "When you leave the room, they immediately start making jokes about you."

After a while I felt a coolness on the part of my colleagues. Nobody came up to me to tell me their problems or to joke around anymore.

They just didn't take notice of me. For some time it was really hard for me but then I thought: Well OK, since you are like that and you can't understand something so simple, then I don't need to socialize with you or talk to you either. And those people who valued me did not reject me.

Sonja: Does your family know you are a lesbian?

Olga: My mother knows but she asked me not to say anything to my brother. She thinks my brother would react badly and his wife has a loose tongue and would make problems. But I think they know because I have a lot of things in my room that reveal it. Sometimes I hear them making jokes about it in general but we have never talked about it openly.

Sonja: Did you want to tell your brother?

Olga: He has so much going on that I don't think he would care. He loves me like a sister. I don't think he would feel differently if he knew I was a lesbian.

Sonja: Does your mother support you?

Olga: Yes, she gives me complete freedom. She does not stop me from being with whoever I like. She helps me a lot.

Sonja: Do you worry about the judgement of society, imprisonment or psychiatric institutions?

Olga: Before, we had to hide this from everyone. Now I feel free. But there are people with whom I cannot be myself, to this day. They simply do not understand me. They don't want to be around me, and I don't want to spoil my relationship with them. As far as psychiatrists are concerned, there was a time when I was being forced to "be cured." But, thank God, I had a good doctor, who spoke well to me and made me feel better. Of course, he advised me to get cured; he gave me an address and said that is was possible to get treated. But at the same time he gave me the idea that I could continue to live like this. Therefore, I never went anywhere.

Sonja: Were you afraid he would have you committed?

Olga: You mean send me to the crazy house? It was actually then that they wanted to put me in one.

Sonja: Who wanted to?

Olga: Oh, it's a long story. I was in love with this girl. I went into a depression and started taking pills. Then because I took too many, I ended up in intensive care. Then when I got better, everything continued in the same vein. Of course, I never told anyone why I did that. There was no one I could really talk to about this. I started taking pills again, and one day I didn't go to work because I couldn't get up from bed. There was a big scandal at work, and they decided I had become a drug addict. They started looking at my veins, checking me all over my body, bringing me to psychiatrists. Many tried to speak with me but I never told anyone what troubled me. I knew it would not be acceptable and they would consider me psychiatrically ill. Obviously they knew something was going on and they decided to try to cure me.

I know what the psychiatric hospital is. They don't cure anyone there. They only make people into morons. I didn't consider myself in any way a moron so I firmly decided not to allow this to happen. I went to that same psychiatrist so that he could treat me, but he spoke nicely with me and said I didn't need to be cured. I felt some kind of foundation or support under my feet.

Sonja: When was that?

Olga: It was four years ago. By the way, my mother, during that time, was very upset and worried. She felt there was something wrong. I found this out from my girlfriend, Olga, who I really loved. I found out that my mother called her, crying, and started reading her my poems, asking her advice. Together they decided what I should do. Then my mother went into town to the psychiatric clinic, got me an appointment card, gave it to Olga to give to me. I confessed to her [to Olga] that I had loved women since childhood, and that I loved her. She handed me the card to go get my cure. It was clear to me she did not get it, nor did she get that I did not think anything was wrong with me. I knew that she would never understand me and would never love me the way I did her. Nevertheless, I thanked her. I threw the card away and said thank you.

Sonja: Did you ever talk about sex with your mother?

Olga: No, never with my mother.

Sonja: When did you first tell her you were a lesbian?

Olga: When I came back from the conference. She said: "Really? I didn't know you had those issues." She reacted pretty calmly and then told me she had started noticing something in the spring: some new girlfriends, running around from here to there, going places, some new interests, long phone calls. Then she happened upon the article in the paper. She knew I had something to do with those people but didn't let on.

Sonja: And how did your grandmother react?

Olga: Oh my snoopy grandmother, going around everywhere, sniffing around, looking through my things, fumbling around... She knows everything but doesn't say a thing.

Sonja: Do you have a desire to come out to society as a lesbian?

Olga: What society? I've already come out. I don't hide.

Sonja: Do you know any older generation lesbians and gays? How do they live?

Olga: I just know people who are five or seven years older.

Sonja: Are you proud of being a lesbian?

Olga: Yes, of course, I consider it being special, "elite" in society. The highest form of woman.

Sonja: Are there any actors, musicians, politicians, who people think are homosexual?

Olga: Yes there are. For example, one singer in Moscow is Sergey Penkin. He even publicly announced on TV that he is gay. He sings well. He is very popular.

Sonja: Any others?

Olga: There are a lot of artists who are not open about it. People know they are gay, they've seen them in our meeting places (*pleshki*), and so forth. They are popular, are known to be gay, but they don't speak publicly about their orientations. But even the way they look, you can easily tell they are gay. I would not have said that before, but now that I've had a chance to hang out with gays, I can recognize their mannerisms and behavior.

Sonja: Would you like to meet one of them?

Olga: Yes, of course I would. I really like Masha Rasputina and Zhanna Aguzarova.

Sonja: Are they lesbians?

Olga: They are singers. They don't say anything publicly. There are lots of gay singers. They're very interesting. I'd love to interact with any of them.

Sonja: You have a picture of Alla Pugachova on your wall. Talk about her.

Olga: I don't want to talk about her because you can't say *only* a few words about her. For me it's an entire life. From her songs, interviews, and press conferences I have learned so much. I can't say whether she is bisexual, although that has been said about her. I do know a girl who apparently was with her. I don't know if one can trust those kinds of stories. On the one hand, it's like gossip. Judging by her behavior, by her freedom, she's probably bisexual. It's very well known that she loves gay men. She has her own theater and she attracts those kind of young men. She lives half the year with a gay man.

Sonja: Tell me a little about what you write.

Olga: My poems take a long time to germinate. It is often very hard to find the right words for feelings, for what goes on inside. Even when you are talking to your beloved and you want to say something to that person, often you can't find the right words, the words you need.

Sonja: Do you write slowly?

18

Olga: It depends. Sometimes it comes out quickly in ten minutes but no poem comes from nowhere, just like that. Underneath, ideas ripen, words come together. Without much notice, perhaps. Then suddenly there is a feeling, maybe grief, I don't know. Sometimes a half a year passes. There is an idea but something is missing, some kind of catalyst, a nudge, a need to bring the thought to a conclusion.

Sonja What do you write about? Women?

Olga: I write about my feelings. I try not to name or focus on a particular woman because with feelings, it's not important if it's a particular woman. And for those who are going to read my poetry, it also wouldn't matter.

Sonja: Tell me about the woman you love.

Olga: Really? From beginning to end? Two years ago she came to work on our shift. My attention was immediately drawn to her. She was a real looker, always neat and presentable. She always looked fresh and clean. She was olive-skinned, interesting. She also paid attention to me right away, because I am the most fun one in the group. Walking around all the time, joking, laughing. I joke around with everyone.

Sonja: So she worked with you?

Olga: Yes, she still does.

Sonja: And what is she?

Olga: Also a *feldsher*, like me. Right away she picked me out of everyone. We started hanging out, talking, going for a smoke together. We'd laugh. She would say: "Let's go stay at my place!" I would say, " Sure." I was a little scared of her but it was nice that she saw me as special and not like the others. She praised me and said I did good work and that I was the smartest one in our station. She and I often discussed medical questions. She liked it that I would argue and not simply agree.

One day we were celebrating Christmas in a restaurant. We talked for a long time, and smoked. Then she asked me to go home with her. I said, "No, I don't want to. Why complicate everything?" First of all, I was afraid of her. Also, she was not a lesbian. She just liked me. If I started coming onto her, she might think—is she crazy? So I thought, better not, just forget it.

She kept at it, "Come on, let's go." I said, "Only if you'll sleep with me." She said OK.

We went to her place. She made my bed in one room and she had hers in another. I said, "No, no, that's not what we agreed on. You promised!" She: "Yeah? Well, OK!" And then she just threw herself at me. It turned out she was very passionate and she wanted me so badly. I was at my wit's end. I didn't know what to do. It was a complete shock to me.

I got very scared, like a child. She expected some very concrete things from me and wanted to do the same to me. But I couldn't do anything, I just got scared to death, and I didn't let her do anything either. I was really stupid. I had no idea what to do with this delight that was unexpectedly thrust on me.

After that, for some time, we kept on a warm relationship, and no sex, as previously. I worried a lot—that she would want me but I wouldn't want her, that she was too old for me. She was twice my age, fifty-two. And as far as sex goes, it seemed like I knew nothing and couldn't even feel anything.

When I came home from Moscow and openly said I was a lesbian, she demonstratively turned away from me. She stopped saying hello to me and in general gave the impression she wanted nothing to do with such a pervert. She was afraid that at work they would think we had been having some sort of relationship and that was why she demonstratively turned away. I never gave anyone any reason to gossip, so it was silly for her to be afraid.

From that time on, we continued to have strained relations. But she never saw me do anything bad. Whatever she needed from me, I did for her, whatever it cost me—money or energy. She never even needed to ask me for anything. I would guess what she needed. She always knew I would do anything for her and would never ask for anything in return. Evidently, that calmed her down.

Then her husband died. Not long before that, maybe a month, I had written her a letter, such a letter, like confessing my love for her. I didn't know if I could ever give it to her, so it lay there in my home for a month. I knew that she was having a hard time, but many others didn't think so. They were saying she didn't love her husband, that she did not have a good relationship with him. But I knew she was very close to him and that he did not fulfil her needs. She didn't have anyone to talk to or to socialize with. I sent her that letter, then I wrote another one. I wrote that I loved her very much, that I knew it was a difficult time now, but maybe the thought that she was loved would help her overcome her difficulties. When she read it, she said it was hard for her to understand all those things. We talked for a long time, including about her intimate life. She said she had never talked with anyone about this before and that it was difficult and unpleasant. Her husband did not satisfy her sexually but she never thought about any other men; she had not wanted to betray him and considered that beneath her. She agonized over this and didn't know what to do, then went to see a sex therapist. Someone suggested to her that since she was not interested in men, maybe she could try women. That thought had never come to her mind. She did not want any woman, and said to me she did not know what had pushed her in my direction.

But I am sure she was not being completely honest with me. I don't think she was trying me out, just like that, out of curiosity. She definitely wanted me—that was clear. And she said I was her first and last woman, that she didn't really like the fact that it was not for her, and she apologized for giving me any expectation of anything.

As you can imagine, it was very hard for me to hear that. It was her initiative. She undressed me and took me to bed and then turned away, saying she was not that kind of person, that it was perverted and those kinds of things. Well, then, how in the world did it all happen? She was such a rational person, always thinking before she acted. I just couldn't get it straight in my head. How did I end up in her bed? To this day I cannot stop wanting her.

Of course she is not a lesbian. But I couldn't help thinking: if I had only given her what she wanted that night and if she had given me what she wanted to give me, she would not be saying this now. I simply did a really stupid thing. For her, it was so difficult to take that step, to decide to do that thing. Then, when she did not get why she did that, she had nowhere else to go but backwards. You can't really go back. She thinks of me as a good person, but all the same our relationship remains cool. She told me that when I came back from the conference, everyone was talking and laughing at me, making jokes at my expense. She also believed it was a perversion and that people shouldn't be that way.

Then after some time, she actually changed her mind. Now she is ready to admit that those kinds of relationships do exist, that gays and lesbian have a right to live the way they see fit. She realizes that they have their own lives, their own problems. That one shouldn't think lightly about these issues inasmuch as their lives depended on all this.

But she could never accept my love. She would say, "Oh my God, look at all the beautiful young women around you! Why would you latch on to an old woman like me? You're just crazy." I'd say to her, "You're beautiful." And she'd say, "No, it's not right. I'll never understand you and I don't want to try. There won't ever be anything!"

Sonja: Does she ever call?

Olga: No, she doesn't. I call her sometimes. But I always feel afraid calling her. I don't want to talk to her as if I'm trying to get together with her. I'm always so nervous around her. I don't know. I think if I were a little smarter, braver, more interesting, it would change everything. She would become "one of us," because things like that don't simply happen. I mean everything that went on between us. She is just a very tough woman and she will not allow herself to relax and do something she might consider a weakness. But I really like her.

Katya and Masha

Interviewed in 1992
Translated by Sonja Franeta

In 1992, when I came to Tomsk, Siberia for the first time, my friend Natasha wanted me to meet two women who lived on the other side of the river and interview them. They had lived together as a couple for six years in a small one room dormitory-type room (obshchezhitie).

We took the bus to a run-down tenement. A bulldozer stood idle in front of some closed shops between two buildings. Dirt and chunks of concrete extended out, a worn path leading to their building. We walked up the broad cold stairwell surrounded by stained, pea-green walls. Natasha knocked when we got to the door. A slight woman with dyed blonde hair opened it and smiled. Natasha introduced me to Masha. The room was neat and clean but the corners and right side of the room were piled high. The left wall was lined with bunk beds and above them were shelves with boxes and more things.

"Katya went to buy something for us to drink," Masha explained. We sat down and began to talk. In the corner by the door, a curtain concealed their small kitchen area. It was hard to believe that two women and two children lived in a space slightly bigger than my bedroom in San Francisco.

Katya walked in with a cap on, looking as if she had just gotten home from work; she was a little taller and broader than Masha.

"I'm a trained nurse," said Masha. "But in order to get this place I had to get a job in the factory so we could live together." Russians often lived with their parents well into middle age because of housing shortages. Marriage gave one the right to a separate apartment but sometimes a married couple had to wait ten years or more to rent an apartment.

Katya and Masha immediately began setting up for dinner. They brought out a folding table which took up most of the room, and all kinds of wonderful food—chicken, fried potatoes, cucumbers in sour cream, beets with fish, eggs with sour cream, black and white bread. At one point Katya proudly set two small bottles of Pepsi on the table and glanced at me. I knew she had gone out of her way to find them especially for me, the American, so I oohed and aahed. Masha's job was the cooking. I complimented her. They appeared to me very much like a U.S. butch/femme couple. I was soon to have my first lesson in labelling people.

After tea, a wonderful torte, and candy, my friend Natasha said she would go out for a walk and give us time to speak alone. I took out my small tape recorder, but before I could turn it on, they stopped me.

Masha: Well, you see, I don't know how to tell you this but we're not lesbians. We're not ashamed or anything. We just keep to ourselves; we just want to live together and be happy.

Sonja: Please explain.

Masha: You see I am a bisexual. I was married. I could be with either a man or a woman.

Sonja: Do you want to be with a man now?

Masha: Oh, no. And Katya is what we call a trans. This is a person who wants to be the opposite sex, a person who dresses like and plays the role of the opposite sex in the relationship.

Sonja: I still want to interview you. Some couples in the United States are like you. Tell me a little about yourselves.

Masha: I was born in the North. After I finished school, I worked in the countryside in a hospital. I was married and had two children when I met Katya. After we met we dated for a while. Then there was a scandal. I moved to my mother's place in Tomsk. A little later Katya came and we began living together.

Katya: I was born in Norilsk then we moved closer to Tomsk. I had a girlfriend before Masha. She lives nearby. I sometimes visit her. We've known each other nine years. When I was eighteen and she was seventeen, we fell in love. But her parents forbid us to see each other. They shouted at me and threatened me with the law. They said: we are going to make sure you go to prison. She was underage. Then I had another woman, older, she was thirty-three. It was very hard for me. After finishing school, I went to work as a streetcar driver.

Sonja: How many years have you been together?

Katya: Six years. We met in 1986. Two months later Masha left her husband. First we lived with her mother, then we lived in an *obshchezhitie* [dormitory or communal housing], a different one.

Masha: My husband's reaction was awful. He ran after Katya with a knife.

Sonja: How old are you?

Katya: I'm twenty-seven.

Sonja: What did you feel when you met?

Katya: I just wanted to live in my own way. It didn't work out for me before.

Sonja: How did you get into the *obshchezhitie*?

Masha: We always had problems getting a place to live. I had to change my job to one that came with a place to live. I went there and with great difficulty I was able to get a place and live separately from my mother. My mother had a small two-room apartment and my sister and her husband and their two children lived there. It was too crowded. My mother doesn't know about me and Katya.

Sonja: Your mother doesn't know? And what about your sister?

Masha: My younger sister knows. I have another sister. The older one is forty. She doesn't know but she has guessed about us. She is not opposed to it for now. I haven't said anything directly to her. I myself am a very independent person. I am sure I won't have any conflicts with them. My mother is old and has health problems. She has no interest in all this.

Sonja: Masha, have you felt attracted to women before?

Masha: No, nothing like this. I never thought anything like this might happen. I felt it only after I had my two children, although I went into marriage without being in love and felt almost nothing. I didn't even understand myself. When Katya and I had to part for a while, it was so hard for me, so sad to separate from her. And then when she started visiting me again, I was so happy; my heart was beating so hard. I could even sense when she was coming or not. We lived in the next village. Then I realized that this was really love and it didn't mean anything that she was a woman. I never had the thought that it was wrong, that it was something bad, not normal. No, I didn't feel that.

Sonja: Are you happy with your choice?

Masha: Yes, I am happy because I feel better about myself than many other women do.

Sonja: Do you feel lonely?

Masha: Only when we argue, when I feel the wall of misunderstanding. But when we make up, and explain things to each other, then everything's OK.

Sonja: Is there any violence in your relationship?

Katya: No, no. We have very tender feelings, no violence, nothing of the sort.

Masha: Of course, sometimes you are jealous.

Katya: Yes, it happens.

Sonja: Do you have any specific roles when you have sex?

Masha: I have the passive role. Katya has the active.

Katya: That's how it is. But we have no problems with sex. At one time, though, I wanted to have an operation.

Sonja: What do you mean?

Katya: An operation to change my sex. Exactly a year ago. They talked me out of it, not so much talked me out of it, but they told me there would be problems or side effects.

Masha: There's no guarantee after the operation everything would be OK.

Katya: It's not very developed here. It's kind of experimental.

Sonja: Do you still want an operation?

Katya: I don't really, now, but I wanted one before. I am trans. I found a specialist but then I decided not to do it.

26

Sonja: What does trans mean for you?

Masha: Lesbians consider themselves primarily women.

Katya: They keep their femininity... if we can judge by our friends who are lesbians.

Masha: But Katya fulfils the role of a man in the house, and in general in our relationship she has chiefly all the male duties: she does all the handiwork—hammering and fixing. And I do the women's work, cooking and laundry.

Sonja: We have similar situations but we call this "roles." It's very common.

Masha: So your lesbians don't want to change their sex?

Sonja: Some lesbians want to play the male role and others want to have the female role but we don't consider them trans.

Katya: I would like to say, that I have had all this since childhood. I don't know how to explain it better. I couldn't wear women's clothes. They said to me: but you are a girl, why are you dressing like that? My mother kept going after me trying to put bows on me, trying to put a dress on me. And I was ashamed. I never wore a dress. I tried not to do what I didn't want. I just couldn't do it. And since childhood I was attracted to girls.

Sonja: And what about work? How are things at work?

Katya: I have chosen the kind of work where you don't have to wear women's clothes. For example, I was driver. Here women drivers wear pants.

Sonja: What do you think of bisexuals?

Masha: Well, I'm a bisexual person. I lived with a man.

Sonja: Do you still want to live with a man?

Masha: No, not now. I consider bisexual women to be those who can live with a lesbian and with a regular man.

Sonja: Do you think there are more bisexual women in Russia than lesbians?

Masha: Yes. We have a lesbian friend. She married a man twice. She just can't understand herself because she is still attracted to both men and women. She lives in the countryside and doesn't really open up about this to anyone.

Sonja: What is your job?

Katya: I drive an electric vehicle in a factory. I deliver things.

Sonja: How is the pay, not great?

Katya: Before they paid more, now the pay is pretty low.

Sonja: And, Masha, where do you work?

Masha: In a different factory, I operate a small crane.

Sonja: Does anyone know about your relationship?

Katya: A very small circle of friends. At work nobody knows. There are only some older people who work there. They wouldn't understand anyway. We say we are sisters.

Masha: Yes, yes, sisters. Sometimes they ask me; why is she so strange, that one? I tell them she is just very athletic, she does a lot of sports. When people do sports their physique changes, and they become more male.

Sonja: What kind of plans do you have for the future?

Katya: If we had the chance, I would love it if we could go to the countryside and grow a garden. The children get sick a lot. Here in the city there is nothing but bad air to breathe. And there are problems at work. You can't get a job in your specialty anyway. Masha wants to work in medicine again. She wants to work in a hospital. But she can't try to get a job in her specialty because then she won't have this place to live anymore.

Sonja: So she is working out of her profession because of this apartment?

Katya: And she makes very little money.

Sonja: Masha, do you have any problems because Katya lives with you?

Masha: No one knows of our relationship. I say she's my sister. I live with my sister. This room is twelve square meters and I have two children. By law, I cannot register her [Katya] here. I have to think about the main problem which is raising and feeding my two children.

Katya: Yes feeding them is not easy.

Masha: Many people have that problem now.

Sonja: And how is everything working out with your kids?

Katya: For now it seems OK. It's only Seryozha, Masha's son, who is kind of curious—he wants to know what, why. We are kind of afraid of this, we want him to have the right understanding of all this. We don't want this to affect him adversely.

Sonja: You think this can have a bad effect on him?

Katya: We keep trying to explain things to him. Nadia is still small. You saw her.

Masha: She sometimes calls Katya "Papa" because from the time Nadia was born Katya has lived with me. She has already gotten used to her. I tell her, that is not your papa. That is Aunt Katya. I try. So they will have the right orientation and know who is auntie and who is uncle. When my son grew up he would ask, "Why is that? Why does Auntie Katya go around in pants all the time?" I tell him I also go around in pants and I'm a woman.

Then in our newspaper they started publishing sections of the sexual encyclopedia, an American one. I started reading it to him and explaining everything—what are the differences and so on. Now he doesn't ask about those things.

Sonja: Can you have sex at home normally?

Katya: We try to put the children to sleep early.

Masha: We wait till they are fast asleep. This is not a problem of our relationship but of the conditions of a small place. We don't show our relationship in any way to our children.

Sonja: You don't embrace each other?

Katya and Masha: No.

Masha: The children don't see anything. It's only at night when they sleep or when they go out, when no one else is home.

Sonja: Yes, I know. It must be difficult. Do you know any favorite actors, any famous actors or singers who are lesbian or gay?

Masha: I like Masha Rasputina. They say she is a lesbian. Also Pugachova, she was very famous. Zhanna Aguzarova.

Sonja: Do you have any desire to come out publicly?

Masha: What would be the point? I don't think anyone would get it.

Sonja: What do you think of the activists in Novosibirsk? They were at the conference in Moscow, they are speaking out in newspapers.

Masha: We are tied down by the children. It's hard to get to Novosibirsk. They are young and energetic, full of optimism. It's easier for them. We have a family and work, other interests and other problems. We have a quiet life. Thank God we found each other. To come out—well, we don't have the desire to, really.

Katya: I had the chance to get to know some of those women in Novosibirsk. I read their article in the paper. I sent them my address and gave them my contact information. I told them I wanted to meet them. And they came here.

Masha: We never had any of this before. Of course, we would like to have more friends and acquaintances. We would like to know that we are not alone. If it wasn't for the newspaper, we would just be living together, the four of us, never knowing about anything else.

Sonja: Did you hear about the Gay and Lesbian Symposium and Film Festival?

Katya: Our people went. It's so good that all those people got together and openly discussed our issues, for example AIDS. They showed them on television several times. They all had "Симпозиум" (Symposium) written on their T-shirts. There was an article about that symposium in the newspaper *Siberian Youth*. The newspaper *AIDS-Info* interviewed them. I saw an excerpt. There was one point when they all got together at the Bolshoy Theater and suddenly started to kiss each other. There was one very sweet couple there. I met them—it was Asya and Lena from Novosibirsk.

Masha: When we are all together, when there are many of us, you feel more courageous, than here, where everyone sits in their own little corner.

Sonja: Do you have gay men friends?

Masha: No, we practically don't know any. We saw some, maybe once. We know Igor Bykov. He's the head of our organization. He put out a newspaper. Actually there are very few of us in Tomsk. You know, people are just afraid of Katya.

Katya: How many times have they said: you are that kind and poked me in the chest, threatening to get me behind bars. You start feeling very insecure.

Sonja: Are you ever afraid of getting raped or violated?

Masha: They beat up Katya with words not fists.

Katya: I have been beaten up physically, too. Her ex-husband.

Sonja: On the street?

Masha: We're not trying to flaunt our lifestyle. People don't come up to us and harass us. We don't provoke people.

Katya: Actually people have become vicious in general. They'll beat you up for not looking at them right, never mind that you're a lesbian.

I would love to have a calmer attitude about myself. Every day I encounter meanness and rudeness. I am constantly getting looks from people. They say, "What is that?" People don't get it. To my face, they just say, "What are you?" They start to argue. That's what they say, "Let's argue about what you are." I can't do anything about it. A few times I tried killing myself but I couldn't do it.

We can't accept what's supposed to be normal. What they think is normal is a man with a woman or a woman with a man and nothing different. It will take many years before they can relate to gays and lesbians at least with tolerance. There is only one reply for them, "Why are you going nuts over this? What's it to you?" They don't understand that this is not just someone's whim, this is not something a person chooses. Do they think we are making this up because we have nothing else better to do?

Sonja: Do you think sexual minorities will become more open?

Masha: People won't ever understand. They'll always be pointing fingers at us. Outcasts.

Katya

Interviewed in 1995
Translated by Sonja Franeta

Katya was born in 1965 in Norilsk, in the far north of Russia. She works in a factory and is trans (transgender). When I interviewed her the first time in 1992, she was with her girlfriend, Masha, and they both participated. They have since separated. The next time I met with Katya, in 1995, she agreed to give me a second interview, which was videotaped.

In her early thirties now, Katya has matured and grown more confident. She says that she has come to accept herself more: becoming acquainted with others who identify as sexual minorities has helped her. (While speaking of herself as trans, she consistently used feminine pronouns and feminine verb endings for herself, as well as a woman's name.) At the end of the interview she took up her accordion and sang some songs with Vera, her new girlfriend.

Sonja: Katya, tell me about yourself. I know that you were born in Norilsk. How did your parents get there? It's very far north. Did they go on their own?

Katya: Yes, they did. They were young. They met there and got married but they were not in Norilsk for very long. The northern climate did not agree with my brother—it was bad for him there—so when I was only a few months old, we moved close to the city of Tomsk.

Sonja: Do you have a big family?

Katya: I have an older brother and a sister. I am the youngest.

Sonja: What did your parents do?

Katya: My father worked as a chauffeur for a long time; then when his health got worse, he went into the police. He got very sick. Mama also worked—in the parks. Now she is retired and rests.

Sonja: Were you young when you realized you were not like other girls?

Katya: I have fallen in love with girls ever since childhood. I fell in love often; I was attracted to them.

Sonja: When did it first happen?

Katya: The first time was with a neighbor girl. That was when we were still in the country. She was about five years older than me. I often went outside. The girls would hang out together at a bench, and I would go out to look at her. Of course, she didn't pay any attention to me. I was still a child. I stood there and just admired her.

Sonja: What happened when you started going to school?

Katya: There I realized, for the first time, who I was and how I was supposed to be. Even then I dressed like a boy, always running around with the boys. It was interesting to be with them. They were always calling me: "Katka, our guy." I almost never wore dresses—it was repulsive to me to wear them. I was abused and even punished. My parents would say, "What is this? Why would a girl dress like this?" But I couldn't do otherwise. I would answer: "If you don't let me wear what I want, I am not going out." At school, of course, I had to wear a student uniform, according to regulations. These days you can go to school in whatever you want. In those days, in the 1970s, it was very strict. Girls could only wear dresses with an apron.

One day they told us: Tomorrow is a holiday. Boys can come in white shirts, dark pants and jackets, and girls in uniforms with white aprons and with bows in their hair. If you do not dress like this, you will be sent home. I came home very upset, not knowing what to do. I told my mother I needed a bow. But I had short hair! All the same, in the morning she made me a bow, but I didn't go to school. To be honest, I walked to school but didn't go in. On the way, I took off the bow and played hooky. I was embarrassed. In general I was a good student. I was an A student all the way up to sixth grade.

Sonja: Did you feel alone at that time?

Katya: Yes I was lonely and it was very difficult. My parents did not even suspect what kinds of problems I had. There were times when I did not even want to live. A few times I tried to kill myself. Even when I was a little girl, I would calm myself down and say: I'll grow up and the doctors will think of something and they'll give me an operation. Then, I actually tried to do this. It became clear, that it would be too expensive, complicated, and not good for my health, so I never decided to do it. It turns out I am not the only one like this.

Sonja: Tell me about your first love.

Katya: Her name was Tanya. We met by chance. I was eighteen and she was seventeen. We saw each other for a long time. She was studying at the Institute, and I was working and living in the countryside with my parents. She came to stay with me on weekends. Sometimes she even skipped her classes because we could not be apart. First, her father found out about everything. Actually, she told him herself and he seemed sympathetic. He said: "OK, I'll let you go and stay over with her." But when her mother found out, she came to see me and created a big scandal. Then her father came and said to me: "Leave my daughter alone, otherwise..." They both got me really scared and said their daughter was a minor. I answered: "How can I promise to leave her alone? You can't dictate to your heart!" Isn't that right?

We saw each other anyway. Her mother then took her to another town and put her into a different Institute. We wrote to each other. They told her bad things about me—that I was seeing others, that it was useless to wait for me. Tanya had a hard time and tried to forget about all that. She proposed we live together on condition that I get an operation. "Let's get you an operation! Then we can get married. We'll live normally. I cannot go against my mother, against my parents. They can't take this. They'll never understand." Now she lives here, nearby, alone. She has a one-bedroom apartment.

Sonja: Do you relate to one another?

Katya: We are friendly. I visited her recently. We have known each other twelve years already.

Sonja: You identify as trans. What do you mean by that?

Katya: In my heart I feel that I am a man, and I dress like a man. Of course, on the outside I look more like a woman and my voice gives me away. Nevertheless, on the street I am often seen as a man. I've been offered a smoke; they curse in my presence.

Sonja: Do you like to be taken for a guy?

Katya: I'm not offended. For god's sake, I dress that way. I don't feel like a woman. Don't you have people like that? I know there are. My partners don't treat me like a woman. When I lived with Masha, I was regarded as man. Even before our acquaintance I would always introduce myself as Oleg. I like that name. They say it suits me. When I was younger, girls gave me the eye. Yes, they would look me up and down. I would meet them and get invited over to their homes.

Sonja: When was that?

Katya: Before I was twenty. I felt freer at that time, more relaxed. It was a happier time, simpler. After twenty, I started to get more introverted, more insecure. What can I do? I can't change how I feel, no matter what. It's part of me.

In general, I am respected for persevering. I mean if you could be in my skin for even five minutes, it's just so difficult! Even for five minutes. At work, I'm a performer. I play Katya, the Woman. Of course, I play the role. I feel relaxed only when I am home and in my circle of friends, not very many. I always end up going into some kind of shell.

Sonja: What words did people use for you when you were small?

Katya: What did they call me then?

Sonja: Other people and you yourself.

Katya: There were no words. Words such as lesbian, I had never heard. They'd say: why are you dressing up like a guy? My brother was embarrassed about me in front of his friends. They would ask him: what kind of sister do you have?

Sonja: How did you find out you could have an operation?

Katya: I collected clippings from newspapers and magazines. Articles about people who had those operations as early as the 1960s. This was all very secretive and it was very considered rare. I found addresses and telephone numbers. A friend of mine suggested I go to some specialists in Tomsk. I called and made an appointment. As soon as they saw me, they promised to help me right away.

Sonja: What did they propose regarding an operation?

Katya: At that time I was still going out with Tanya, so we went to the consultation together. First Tanya went into the office. The doctors asked her a few questions, like about what I wore. She said a man's down coat in the winter. Interesting, they said. Then they called me in.

I went into the office and there were two doctors—men. They looked me over, exchanged glances and nodded their heads.

They started asking me questions: How do you live? Have you had any encounters with the opposite sex? What did you experience? I explained everything to them. I had a few casual encounters with men but no attractions. I talked about Tanya. The doctor said, "OK. We can help you." These were their recommendations—that I go to a psychiatric hospital for a minimum of two weeks, in order to ascertain that this is not a form of depression or a delirious state and that I am a psychologically normal person. Then they asked if I knew what they would do. They said everything would be artificial. They did not guarantee that my normal sensations would remain. They said there were times when a person who went ahead with this kind of thing changed their mind. It would be necessary to change my passport—first my name, last name, address. I might even have to go away somewhere for a while. I would have to get used to living as someone else for about a year and a half, taking hormones and preparing for the operation. Then, the operations—first one, then a second one. There may be many, perhaps five operations. My health must be excellent. In other words, I'd have to give up everything and go away. I wouldn't see my parents for a while. Everything seemed too difficult. I could not come to a decision. Maybe if I were younger, twenty, perhaps, I would have done it. Now there was no sense in it. I'm doing OK like this.

Sonja: Did the doctors treat you well?

Katya: Yes, they understood me, like no one else. It was obvious they respected me as a person. One was from Moscow the other was one of our own, from Tomsk—a professor and does those kinds of operations. They were honestly trying to help me. I even started to get my work reference to go ahead with it, but then I thought it over. I don't regret it.

Sonja: Tell me about your parents. Where are they from?

Katya: My mom is a German and my father is from Byelorussia. My mother is a Volga German. I know German. On my mother's side everyone is German. They even subscribe to German newspapers. That whole side of the family reads German. My grandmother spoke very little Russian and at home she spoke only German. These days in Russia, Germans are forming communities. If someone has relatives in Germany, they get connected and try to emigrate. My mother is not getting her documents ready, even though I told her to do this a long time ago, since there was a possibility to go. My mother had a lot of relatives and cousins and she was from a big family. There's even an organization of Volga Germans in our city. All of them were victims of repression.

Sonja: Repression? Talk about that.

Katya: I don't know very much about it myself. Many years ago, they used to live around the Volga River, near Saratov. When World War II started, they were all driven out and sent here to Siberia. They had to leave their homes and farms. The Germans used to live well in those villages. They were dispossessed as kulaks and lost everything. They were brought to Siberia with only their personal belongings.

Sonja: Did the children tease you in school?

Katya: They called me a German. I cried and complained. I had a very hard time. Furthermore, they not only called us Germans but Fascists. But we weren't fascists at all; they were just Germans not fascists. Now there's a different attitude and it's easier.

Sonja: What religion was your family?

Katya: Orthodox Christian, I guess. I really don't know for sure.

Sonja: What about their political views? What did they think about communism?

Katya: The same as everyone else at the time. They were kind of confused, tricked. I read one book about this recently—it's called *The Party's Gold* by Igor Bunich ! It's such an interesting book. It puts your hair on end. Amazing, the things the regime did to people!

Sonja: How did you all live? Was it a small village? Did you live in a house or an apartment?

Katya: When I was small, we had our own house in Achinsk. A small brick detached house. We were fine, for the most part.

Sonja: What did your mother think about you?

Katya: My mom thought all this was temporary. Things like that happened. Girls like to wear pants, it's more comfortable. She tried not to pay much attention to it. But now she respects the fact that, despite everything, I am alive and well and I haven't fallen into ruin. I smile no matter how hard life is for me.

Sonja: How about your sister and brother? How do they feel?

Katya: When I was younger my sister related pretty well to me. I already told you about my brother. He was embarrassed by the way I looked, by the fact that I was not like everyone else. Then he changed. When I wanted an operation, I told him everything about myself. It seemed like he understood and would slap me on the back and say, "Hey, brother!" Now he knows everything about me and relates well to me.

Sonja: Did your parents or anyone at school ever suggest that you go to a psychiatrist?

Katya: No, never—only the doctors suggested it before a possible operation. They wanted me to go to the psychiatric hospital but they didn't think I had a psychiatric disorder.

Sonja: What other problems have you had?

Katya: When I lived with Masha, there were problems with her children. She had two children. As they were growing up, they kept asking questions. I sometimes was a little tough with them. Masha would get upset with me. I think two women can create family, but as far as children, I doubt it. They should not be under the influence of our sexual orientation. In the end, Masha herself told me, "Let's end our relationship for the children's sake. My son is growing up and so is my daughter." And that's what we agreed on. We are still friends.

Sonja: How are things at work?

Katya: Now I am working as an electric vehicle driver at the factory. I always worked as a driver, on a trolley, or a streetcar. I like that kind of work. The uniform is also nice for me. I could also see myself as a police officer and I'd like the job of investigator. But there, women have to wear skirts.

Sonja: Do you have problems because of how you dress?

Katya: Of course, there are problems. I try not to stick out. I prefer dressing in sports clothes. They're comfortable and easy. But it's hard here. People are always looking at you. They notice something is not right! A lesbian, probably! We [Russians] are a mistrustful people, dark, you know what I mean?

Sonja: In general, do people relate to you OK?

Katya: Yes, I think so. I work and try hard. They gave me an apartment which is not so easy to get these days. Especially, because of the fact that officially I don't have a family. Here, in this country, it's very hard to get an apartment in this situation.

Sonja: Were there other girls like you in school?

Katya: Like me? I didn't see any at the time. In general, though, of course, there must have been. Where they are now, I don't know. They hide. They're afraid. There are a lot, even in our city. Often, their lives fall apart. It's very hard for people like that to live in our country. I don't know what it's like in your country. Maybe your people are more open. Russians are kind of angry. Especially now, what's going on in this country! Everyone is focused on their own problems; they're all so gloomy. Have you noticed that?

Sonja: Do you have girlfriends? I mean, a circle of friends?

Katya: At first, I never said anything to anyone; I kept everything inside. But now I know I'm not alone. I found the girls from Novosibirsk, who we both know, after reading a news article about them and I wrote them a letter. These days it's much easier for me. However, as before, I don't have many close friends. It's a small circle. There's Natasha, the ones from Novosibirsk. There's also Zhenya. Did you meet her? Do you know who she is? These are the only people I can be really open with, who I can talk to about whatever I want.

Sonja: Do you have a place to meet here? How do you find one another?

Katya: For the most part we meet by chance. For example, I've known Vera a long time. Our parents lived in a village that's not far away. We've gone there together. Her mom relates to me very well, her brothers, and relatives too. It turns out she has always been attracted to me. She would come to see me at my job, back when I was eighteen, and watch me. But I couldn't really take any liberties then. The village is small; everything would be known right away. I could not be open then, and she was afraid to reveal her own feelings. But it's a small world and we met up again here.

Sonja: Do you have any favorite stars—movie actors, and so on?

Katya: Arnold Schwarzenegger. When I do my exercises, I look at this poster. In general, I really like bodybuilding. I train sometimes.

Sonja: You told me once before you liked riding motorcycles. There was a club.

Katya: Yes, I used to ride motorcycles when I was at the factory. It's too bad I was never in a competition. I have ridden motorcycles since childhood, I guess, since second grade. My father helped me and he taught me to fix them too. I sold my motorcycle. I wanted to buy a new one but I don't have a garage to put it in.

Sonja: Do women ride motorcycles here?

Katya: In the countryside where I used to live, I actually taught the neighbor girls how to ride motorcycles. They learned everything and got their licenses. They remember me for this. But in those days it was not ok. Now it's a different time. I would be happy to ride around now.

Sonja: In your opinion, is there a difference between Soviet times and today? Has this change influenced your life?

Katya: We have more information. Today there are stories about people like us even on TV and in the newspapers. Actually, people seem to have more problems now and they have no time to think about us. A job to buy what they need, that's what people are thinking about. As far as the country in general there are not any big changes. For seventy years, Russia carved a path in one direction, and now it's still unclear how everything will turn out.

At work I never talk about my issues with anyone, naturally. They just wouldn't understand me. They all think since I haven't gotten married by age thirty, something's wrong. I don't live like everyone else. That means something is not right. But I am not worried. Let them think what they want and say what they want. Actually, I am quite an emotional person. I worried a lot before and jeopardized my health because of it. Now I decided I don't have to pay any attention, but it's hard. People like me have a terrible time with psychological pressures. They get beaten down, fall apart, and sometimes even kill themselves. The only one choice is to hold on, no matter what.

Sonja: Do you have a better life now than before?

Katya: Yes, it's gotten easier. I've become more experienced in life. I'm already thirty. I don't feel insecure like before. How I hated myself in those days! I wanted to run away into the forest and hide somewhere. How many times I tried to commit suicide! Now I've learned to respect myself, and others too. Everyone has their own life. If I like a person, then well and good. This doesn't concern other people. Live and let live.

Tanya

Interviewed in 1995

Translated by Sonja Franeta

Tanya, an attractive woman with brown eyes and mid-length hair is a Tatar by ethnicity and a businesswoman by profession. She has a confident air and says she does not depend on anyone, neither at work nor in her personal life. During the interview she seemed shy, even though we had known each other beforehand. She wanted to come to my place to have the interview because she wasn't comfortable answering questions at her home.

One interview took place at the well-known OBCOM [Communist Party] Dachas [vacation homes] near Novosibirsk, where she grew up. She pointed out places connected with events she spoke about, for example, where she met her first girlfriend and the dance platform where she danced as a teenager. After the interview she said she expected more personal questions, but they turned out to be more political.

Sonja: Tell me a little about your childhood. Where were you born? What was your family like, and what did your parents do for a living?

Tanya: I was born in the Novosibirsk region. When I was five, my parents found work close to Novosibirsk at the OBCOM [Communist Party] dachas in the village of Sosnovy Bor and we left the big city. In my childhood, I felt my parents were deprived of their rights. They never worked in their areas of specialty: my mother was a trained technician and my father an electrical engineer. They were forced to work there [at the OBCOM dachas] in order to acquire an apartment. They did this for the sake of their children—me and my sister.

My entire childhood was spent at those dachas, a separate territory where party officials relaxed and vacationed. These people were privileged. They were allowed everything and everyone else got nothing. Leaving the premises and even going to the store was allowed only according to a strict schedule. It was a restricted piece of land, and the servants were not allowed to leave it. There was a separate beach for the service people and a separate beach for vacationers. My parents were the servants for these officials and didn't have their own living quarters, so they were promised an apartment in about five to ten years. This always felt oppressive. There were a lot of things like that I don't care to remember. I always thought, why is it like this? Isn't this discrimination? This kind of dependency always upset me. Therefore, later, I always tried to become independent, finish my studies, work, and never depend on anyone.

I was sent to town to go to school, and I went every day for ten years. My mother helped me get to Krasnoyarsk [another large Siberian city] when I finished school. I really wanted to get into the art institute. I always liked drawing. I went to the Institute but I lived in a hotel. The hotel was not really expensive for the times, but my mom thought it was expensive and I did too. I lived and studied in Krasnoyarsk for only three months. Then I decided to give up the Institute and return home. I realized that I should have been getting my education in Novosibirsk and helping my parents. For one year I worked at the Construction Institute as a draftsperson; in the evenings I took preparatory courses. In my free time, I went to Sosnovy Bor and spent time with my peers. I also helped my parents with their chores. We had our own garden and it needed a lot of work. I attended the Novosibirsk Construction Institute and majored in architecture. While I was taking classes, I made some money as an artist. When I finished the Institute, I worked in an architectural studio. Then I got married.

Sonja: Let's talk a little about your ethnic background. Were your father and mother Tatars? Do you know the Tatar language?

Tanya: Yes, I am a full-blooded Tatar. I was born in Siberia. There are Kazan Tatars, Crimean Tatars, and even Siberian ones. In the Novosibirsk region there is a large Tatar settlement. My parents were from there. I was born in the Kolyvanovsky region, in the village of

Kazanka. My very first years I lived with my grandmother. She raised me and for this reason I know the Tatar language and culture very well: our beliefs, customs, holidays, and religion. My parents then took me home with them and when it came time to go to school I didn't know how to speak Russian. This bothered my mother. She wanted me to go to a Russian school, so I had to learn Russian. My mother and father started teaching me. When I went to first grade, I hardly knew any Russian. Nevertheless, I caught up and got excellent grades all the way up to sixth grade. I socialized with my peers and I really liked school. My favorite subjects in school were Russian language and literature. But I continued to go to my grandmother's and there I had a chance to speak Tatar all the time. I like that I was fluent in both languages. It was kind of unique. At the Institute, I also wanted to socialize with people of my own nationality, but my Tatar classmates did not know our language and I was sorry about this.

Sonja: Did the children in school tease you because you were Tatar?

Tanya: No, but there was one episode. One little boy got mad and called me out, then I gave it to him; I was strong enough. The teachers always defended me. Maybe because I was well-behaved and a good student. No one focused on my nationality. I was often praised for how well I learned the Russian language and how interested I was in the literature. There could have been problems—there were Russians everywhere and I was the only Tatar. My mother was an intelligent woman. She always instilled in me not to pay attention to any of that. Therefore, I never had problems with this, neither in school nor at the Institute.

Sonja: Was your family religious?

Tanya: My mother became religious after my father's death. She didn't know the rituals very well, except for what my grandmother taught her, like the basic prayers. After the burial, when she was left alone with two children, she just started asking for help.

Sonja: Are you all Muslim?

Tanya: Yes, we keep the Muslim faith. We don't ask God for things, we only ask for his continuous blessing. When a person gets lucky or when things are bad, they always say [a word in Tatar]. This person only praises God, praises him constantly. However, we didn't have a mosque.

Sonja: Did your parents speak about politics?

Tanya: In Soviet times, it was never talked about out loud. We were not allowed to freely discuss these subjects, even literature was forbidden. Many people were unhappy but they became used to their immediate surroundings. When my parents, in order to get an apartment, ended up with jobs that were not in their specialty, it didn't bother them. What concerned them was me and my sister. Nobody really focused on what was going on in the country overall. And those whose interest was politics often suffered political persecution. Even in the 1980s people were put in prison because of politics. My parents were not interested in this, and neither was I nor my peers. Life was monotonous and tedious. People thought everything was fine, everything was great. The main thing was to have something to eat. Now everything is different. I don't even want to remember those times.

Sonja: What was your family like? You have one sister. How did you relate to her?

Tanya: Yes, she was my older sister. Everything was always very peaceful at home. We all had good family relations.

Sonja: Who did you play with as a child?

Tanya: I played with the children of other service personnel. But I wanted to hang around with other children, because I found some things in common with them. There were a lot of people to hang out with, and in the village there were dances in the evenings.

Sonja: Did anyone in your family speak about sex? Did your mother speak to you about having your period?

Tanya: One day my mom sat me down in front of her and explained what I would go through. I was already thirteen. She explained everything concretely. I remember going to school early in the morning one day and suddenly feeling a change in myself. I had to return home. I had begun my period. It was unexpected but I already knew what it was.

Sonja: In general, do people talk about these things with their children?

Tanya: They probably do now. But before they didn't. I think there were some prejudices. And it was simply ignorance, a lack of education, about all things that concerned sex. There was very little written material. Now parents try to warn children, explain to them what to expect. At that time not very many women could explain this to their daughters. Children grew up with insecurities because of this.

Sonja: Tanya, do you remember your first sexual feelings?

Tanya: Yes, I remember. I fell in love with my first teacher and after that I constantly fell in love with women. Now I understand that one's intimate life depends on a person's taste. But then I didn't know that, and it seem to me that my feelings could have been unnatural. I tried not to think about that. So when I went to Krasnoyarsk and started working I fell in love with a woman. I was only eighteen and she was twenty-eight. Yes, I was crazy in love. Those were most likely my first sexual feelings. We didn't do anything, but the desire for physical closeness was definitely there. I remember that very clearly. My first kisses were with her. The things a person experiences the first time one remembers for the rest of one's life. That person is still important to me to this day.

At that time I was very shy. I got nervous whenever she went away somewhere and I waited for her to return. When we kissed the first time, she said very directly that she wanted me. That surprised me then. How could she talk that way?

Only afterwards, I understood that love was a very individual thing and that desire for physical closeness with a person of the same-sex was normal and natural. At that time I didn't understand. I felt that I was the only one like this. It's so good that today I can socialize with people like me, that I can surround myself with people close to me in spirit.

Sonja: For how long did you have the sense that something was not right with you?

Tanya: Yes, I had that kind of feeling. In school I didn't really fall in love, I simply got very attached to girlfriends. I didn't pay much attention to this at that time. I was studying and had a lot of things to do and many distractions. But when I came to Krasnoyarsk, I ended up having a lot of free time and felt bored. Then I found new girlfriends and befriended only those who attracted me. I couldn't just have friends. Both their looks and their personalities were important. I began to fall in love when I was at the Institute. It didn't just happen once, yet I couldn't open up and say what I was or what I felt. I myself could not even clearly understand what was going on with me. I thought, perhaps I was falling in love with those who I was supposed to be friends with. I was very attached to my girlfriends. In the third year I had a girlfriend with whom I was close until the end of the Institute. Although we were very close friends, I still could not open up to her. She also loved me a lot but then she got married and everything ended.

I have changed a lot since then. Now I am ready for those kinds of relationships. Even my straight friends know that I am a lesbian. I can freely talk about this, but before I couldn't. Before I was lonely.

Sonja: Before, meaning in childhood?

Tanya: No, I was speaking about my time at the Institute and after the Institute. I was starting to have problems with men at the time. The fact is I had no interest in them at all. But in my circle of friends there was no one like me. I was supposed to socialize with men but they never brought up any feelings in me. Nothing resembling the butterflies I experienced with women, which I felt even when I had ordinary encounters.

Sonja: Tell me about your first love affair.

Tanya: I always remember it with great pleasure. She came to the sanatorium to get treatment. She had heart problems. I noticed her immediately, a newcomer. Everybody knew each other there and they pointed out newcomers. I wanted to meet her but I was very unsure of myself. I watched her at the dances, from the sidelines. It was nice to just look at her. And then something wonderful occurred! One day I was sitting at the dance in a corner talking with my friends. I realized suddenly that that girl was dancing only with women. I watched her and thought: well, others are dancing with her, couldn't I also go up to her and ask her to dance? At that moment I picked up my head and she was standing before me asking me to dance. Naturally, I danced with her the whole night. The next day I ran over to the dance and we got to know each other better. She played the guitar and sang. We would go off to the river and spend evenings there. We became friends. We dated, went to town together, went to the theater, to concerts. I was attracted to her but I was only eighteen. I was still very reserved. At the end of the season she left. We wrote each other all winter. Then in the spring she came again. And we started dating again. That went on for three years. But it was not enough. It was not enough for me, personally. Maybe she had a relationship in Omsk. I knew she only had girlfriends there. She was never married. We spoke openly only later. One day in a letter did she say she was afraid she would scare me off. She was very careful when she was with me, afraid she would frighten me, like a butterfly. She wanted to keep everything the way it was so I would have pleasant memories.

Then she stopped coming. I went to the Institute and started a new life. Little by little, we drifted apart from each other. But to this day, we remain friends and write to each other. I get postcards from her. She has her life and I have mine, but I am very grateful to her.

Sonja: When you figured out you were a lesbian, did it worry you?

Tanya: Yes, I went through a lot. At that time people couldn't talk about it. I had a lot of women around me. At times I could kiss one or more of them, yet the next day everything was quickly forgotten. Everyone pretended that it was just an accident. People were afraid to be open. I worried about it a lot. I thought, was it possible I was the only one like this? Is it possible that everything is upside down inside me? Is it only me who loves women? Wasn't there anyone else with mutual feelings? I so much wanted that!

One day, finally, I lucked out. I was working in the Siberian transport office at the Institute and met another girl there. She was a year older than me. We had a lot of similar tastes. We would read together, go to films, the theater. We were together all the time. We got very used to each other. Then one time, I spent the night at her house. We slept in the same bed. I still get butterflies when I think of it. We were afraid to touch each other. I felt there was an energy that came from her and it blended with mine. Very slowly we turned to each other, then firmly embraced. I remember our first kiss. It was something unique!

Later I got to know a woman who was ten years older than me. With her, I was able to have a real sexual experience and I began feeling much freer. We would sleep together, explore one another, and do it all with such pleasure. Despite this, we never went public with our relationship.

Sonja: How did you find out there were other people like you?

Tanya: It was completely by accident. One day I was in someone's house and saw a book by Sappho on the shelf. I started reading her poetry and I realized the poems were about her love for women. I was, so to speak, inspired with new life. I wanted to know who the book belonged to and it turned out it was the host's. This was the first person I could talk to about this subject. I got together and talked with him often for the next two years; this was the only man I could relax with, because I saw that he was close to me in lifestyle. He had a boyfriend and I could come to his home with my girlfriend. It was really nice.

Sonja: Was he gay?

Tanya: Yes, but he was not public about it. Nobody knew that about him. His work was very important to him and he was afraid to be open. We were very happy that we met each other, thanks to Sappho. We read poetry out loud. We looked for other books on the subject. At that time you could actually find a few things. We spent interesting times together.

Sonja: Do you have more women friends or more male friends?

Tanya: Women. It was always more interesting for me to spend time with women.

Sonja: How did lesbians meet each other back then? How did they recognize each other? Were there any places where women could meet each other?

Tanya: No, there were no places like that. When I first realized I was a lesbian I felt sorry I couldn't openly socialize with everyone I wanted to. Only I and my girlfriend went around together. If my girlfriend and I kissed and hugged, I would get blank stares. In the summer, we would go to the workers' camp to work. Boys were interested in us. They'd invite us to get together in the evenings and we got nervous. But we went and we tried to make friends with them. She went to one side and I to the other. When we finished, we'd walk back together on the dark streets, wander around, sit on the riverbank, hug and kiss each other, cry and say: "Oh my God! Who wants all them? We're just fine when it's just the two of us!" Now could I say this to anyone. At that time, we were secretive.

Sonja: Did you tell your mom and your sister?

Tanya: No, I have never yet said anything about it to them. I would love it if one of them found out, even if it was difficult. Many of my friends know, even some of my colleagues know. But my family does not. Maybe my mother has figured it out. She never gave the impression that this would surprise her in anyway, even if something was going on with me. But she never asked me about anything. She always said, "If it's meant to be, you'll tell me everything!" My sister has her own problems. She has a husband and three children and I think my life doesn't interest her very much. But of course I would like to tell them about everything.

Sonja: Do you think you will?

Tanya: Maybe. They're all so interested in my having a partner, a better half. I don't like these questions. Probably I will tell them, but they're my only family. I just don't know if they'll understand me or not.

Sonja: Do they know about you at your job?

Tanya: At work with my coworkers it's also difficult. For example, when they ask you to come over to their homes. Do you go there alone or with a girlfriend? There could be family people there with traditional views. They may say out loud, or to themselves, that it would be better if Tanya came with her partner! Of course what they have in mind is with a man. I don't want to have to explain things to people, but sometimes I have to. I end up saying that men only interest me as friends. Probably if I had come out earlier I would be freer, more relaxed. But everything started pretty late for me. Only now do I understand what has been holding me back and what stops me to this day. I have become another person, a person who can open herself up every day.

Sonja: What do you think about those who publicly talk about their sexual orientations? Do you know the term coming out?

Tanya: Yes, I know it. To be open about yourself. To openly talk about this. I think it is great. I've always been envious of those people. We now have some leaders who want to organize something and get together to discuss our issues openly and do something to better our situation. I would like to take part in this now.

Sonja: What about your job? Did the fact that you are a lesbian affect your choice of work?

Tanya: No, it didn't affect my choice. For a while I worked in a construction institute. I designed apartment buildings and children's playgrounds. I was very happy to do my work on interiors and choose equipment for the children.

At the beginning of the nineties, when Russia started to have inflation, it was very hard to live on the salary I got. I realized I had to be more independent and organize my own business. I got loans and started a business that involved selling food products. It was very difficult but I worked and I still work independently. Of course I would like to have more money and, in the future, to do some good for the city. My dream is to have my own architecture studio. But it turns out I have to wait, because for that you need a lot of money.

Sonja: Did you ever come across any gays or lesbians at work? How did you deal with that?

Tanya: Sometimes. I'd use my intuition and could tell if they were. But I can't really talk about it with them. Not long ago, there was this situation. I went into an office and saw a young man at the counter, taking orders. I knew right away that he was one of us. I wanted to talk to him. I asked if he knew a certain person, as a way to check if I was right about him. Perplexed, he looked at me and was at a loss. He said, no he didn't know him. Then I thought: how sad that people to this day could not just be open about themselves and talk honestly. I left with a feeling of regret and sadness that I couldn't find a commonality with him. This happens quite often. Obviously there are still a lot of insecurities. People live hidden by codes. They're afraid to lose their jobs, or spoil their lives.

Sonja: Are you not afraid?

Tanya: No, I am not afraid now. I am ready for anyone to ask me a direct question; I'll answer that I love women. I don't need to be hypocritical or to lie. This is how I can feel much better about myself. There was a time when I was asked, why are you always with women? At first I would answer: "that's my own private business and shouldn't interest anyone else." I never made up stories, such as I have a husband or my best guy is on a trip, like some people do. Now I just say directly that men don't interest me.

I don't have any problems with my intimate life. I feel like a complete human being. To fall asleep and to wake up with my beloved woman gives me both spiritual and physical pleasure. The question: "do you need a man?" for me just doesn't exist.

Sonja: Do you use the word lesbian?

Tanya: Before I might have hesitated. But now I've gotten used to it, for me it's part of my culture, it means family.

Sonja: What kind of words did women use before?

Tanya: They would use *goluboy* (blue), *rozovaya* (pink). I learned about them later. I guess there are other words, too. I just don't know them.

Sonja: Are you familiar with the terms active and passive [top and bottom]? What do you think of these?

Tanya: I have felt both ways. But I don't like those kinds of divisions. I love the word woman, I feel very much a woman. When you make love, you really want everything to be mutual. That's the only way to receive satisfaction. But that doesn't happen all the time.

Sonja: What do you think of transgender people? Do you socialize with them?

Tanya: I have one friend like that. I can talk to them. But it's not what I want. I need a woman.

Sonja: Have you ever had problems with the law because you're a lesbian? Do people have those problems here?

Tanya: Yes, there are problems but I think this happens only because of people's stupidity. Now nobody can declare that the way of life I lead is not normal or not natural.

Sonja: Did you ever go to a psychiatrist?

Tanya: Thank God, no. It never even entered my mind. The feelings that I have had were always pleasant to me and I never wanted to get rid of them. Only a person who is tortured by doubts would go to a psychiatrist, a person who's unstable and weak.

Sonja: Have you heard that some women have been sent to psychiatric institutions because they are lesbians?

Tanya: No, I never heard that. Maybe I just never came across it.

Sonja: Do women go to prison for this?

Tanya: No, I don't think so. Women go to prison for completely different reasons. But it happens that when a woman goes to prison, she connects with people she has never known before; she may have an experience and then doesn't turn it down. I know someone like this. She was married and had three children. In the camp she met a woman and that woman gave her much more than her husband ever did. This way of life became much closer to her. She left her family and her children, all because of this woman. She got divorced officially, right there in prison and no one judged her at that time. Maybe this happened quite often in the gulag.

Sonja: Were you married?

Tanya: Yes, it's a very sad story, an unfortunate episode. The only mistake I made in my life was to get married to a man. I didn't do it for love. Maybe I was bound to this person somehow. If there was a choice at that time, either to get married or to meet a woman, I would have immediately rejected getting married. Now all of this looks humorous to me. But at that time I went into it very consciously. I thought, let me get married and I'll compare. A person has to go through that too, probably. But being married did not give me any satisfaction. Although I did get some important life experience because of it. He helped me, once and for all, to reject men.

We divorced more than four years ago. We separated as friends. I told him that I would never get married again. He was not a stupid man and understood things himself.

Sonja: Did you have children?

Tanya: I think I got married because I wanted a child. But my husband had problems. We tried for three years and he went into treatment but it was useless. Now I think it was probably for the best. Obviously, it's no longer the time for me to have a child. And now, how would it happen? Only with the help of a clinic.

Sonja: Do you think women have a secondary position in society?

Tanya: Maybe that's the way it was before but now women who have their own businesses are very independent. There are also women leaders, with professional backgrounds. They know how to handle themselves. I've seen this over the past two or three years. Men have learned to yield to these women. However, in earlier times women have been considered strong, especially as supervisors. But along with this came the idea that this kind of woman was not quite a woman. For some reason the weak, dependent women became appreciated the most. Now everything is different.

Sonja: How do people regard a woman leader who is a lesbian?

Tanya: I could possibly see, but others wouldn't. Or else, perhaps, they'd close their eyes to it. Also, she would not allow anyone to say something bad about her.

Sonja: What world events or events in Russia have affected your life?

Tanya: In Russia, the current changes can only bring joy. I think that the changes have given people of my generation and those younger than me many incentives. I would not like to return to the old days. I want to live openly and liberated.

Sonja: What was bad about the old days?

Tanya: At that time I wouldn't have had what I have today. I had fewer friends, and basically they were heterosexual. That's the first thing. Secondly, complete freedom at work. I can work the way I want and I can allow myself anything, as long as there is money. Before, even basic food products were only available with ration tickets. And you couldn't really make money, only a limited salary.

Sonja: What else can you say about your life?

Tanya: My life isn't that easy. I find myself in humiliating situations. One night, a taxi driver took me very much out of the way from where I was supposed to go to. He said: "I am not going any further—you go yourself." I took these kind of things very hard. They affected my relationships with men in general. I realized that I had to be independent. I worked a lot, so that I could have my own car. I took out a loan. I decided that the first big purchase I would make would be a car. Now I can get to places on my own, wherever I want. I don't have to ask anything of a man. I can do it all myself.

Sonja: Is it unusual for a woman to have a car?

Tanya: Now, no. But I was compelled to do this because of incidents like the one with the taxi driver who left me there at night.

Sonja: What kind of hopes and dreams do you have for the future?

Tanya: To get satisfaction from my work. Have a good personal life. When everything is going well for you, you don't want to think about tomorrow and plan things. I don't plan things. I live. I only plan vacations and trips. And work. Everything else is fine.

Sonja: Do you like to travel?

Tanya: Yes, I do. The last two years I never went anywhere, I just worked. I had such short vacations. I want to go to some civilized city. Somewhere out of the country. I want to relax, either alone or with my loved one.

Sonja: Do you want to add anything else? Or share anything about your life?

Tanya: Now, I'm just happy. Happy that I'm a lesbian. I think that people should live the way they want, not try to change themselves. Many women cannot come to terms with this. They think that if they fall in love with a woman, it's not okay. But it really doesn't matter for whom you have that feeling. If you live with a loved one, everything will be great.

Igor

Interviewed in 1995
Translated by Lara Ravitch
Edited by Sonja Franeta

Tall with a slender face, Igor was born in Krasnoyarsk in 1952. Beginning in 1990, he organized a social group for gays and lesbians in town. In the interview he explains some little known facts, including the work of the Special Department [of the police] in "the struggle against sexual crimes." This campaign by the police instilled fear among gays in several large Siberian cities in the 1980s.

Sonja: Tell me a little about your background.

Igor: I'm of Polish descent, actually Belorussian-Polish. My father was Polish, and my mother was Belorussian. My father's ancestors were resettled in the Krasnoyarsk Region during the Tsarist times, and my mother's parents during the Soviet era. I don't know how true that is. They think they were descendants of Polish nobles. My father's ancestors lived in Bogotulsky Region, in the same settlement where other exiled Poles were. Then my mother's father was sent to Krasnoyarsk Region as the first secretary of the party's Kondinsky District Committee. He worked there.

Sonja: Do you speak Polish?

Igor: No, only my grandmother on my father's side spoke Polish, and not very often. She also sang Polish songs. You know, in our house we sang in Ukrainian and Belorussian. I even remember one of the songs, but I don't sing, myself.

Sonja: Did you ever have problems because of your heritage?

Igor: I didn't personally. All my documents say I'm Russian. That's how they did it then. I have a friend whose father is Georgian and her mother is half Georgian, but her passport says she's Russian, too. You know, I never identified as Polish. I went to a Russian school and spoke Russian, so I'm Russian.

Sonja: How did your family feel about communism?

Igor: My mother's father was a Communist to the marrow of his bones; he was secretary of the regional council in Stalin's time. Our family wasn't affected by any repressions, except for once. This was already after Stalin died, under Khrushchev. Cattle had died in the region that my mother's father managed so, until the end of his life, he had to pay for the cost of the herd. It didn't matter whose fault it was. He thought that was to be expected. A true communist! And the people who were resettled didn't protest, didn't get outraged, no matter how bad their living conditions were.

Sonja: Were you instilled with communist ideals when you were a child?

Igor: Yes, I was raised in the spirit of socialism. I was a revolutionary scout, then a Pioneer [communist youth group], and not just a member. Before I was fourteen, I became representative to the Council of Friendship from the Krasnoyarsk region. The Council of Friendship was the regional leadership of the Pioneers. I was a representative to that council. Then, naturally, I became a *Komsomolets*, member of the primary school Komsomol council, and then a member of the high school Komsomol [older youth group] council. I led my freshman group, and they looked up to me. I never heard any negative comments about the socialist system in my family. Actually, where would they have come from? On the one hand, my mother's father was a party leader and he didn't suffer any of the repression. And on the other, he didn't get any special benefits either, not for him nor his family. He had six children. When the family moved from one region to another, which happened a lot, they went on their own dime, not the Party's, and they rode in third class [on the trains], the cheapest. My mother has an older sister, who's still a fervent Stalinist. Whenever something happens, she declares: "If only Stalin were here!"

Sonja: Did your family adhere to any kind of religion?

Igor: My grandmother on my father's side was Polish, and a practicing Catholic. I spent most of my time with her and she insisted that I get baptized. She was very pious, observed all the fasts and holidays. At that time in our city, there wasn't any Catholic community; there was only the Orthodox Church. They took me to Belorussia when I was only a little over two. They baptized me there, near Brest. My father was baptized, too. My grandmother on my mother's side, although she was baptized in the Orthodox Church, was not a believer. My mother was not baptized; she was the daughter of a Communist, although she never joined the Party. In general, I couldn't say that my family had a negative opinion of religion.

Sonja: Are you an only child?

Igor: Yes, just me. I'm selfish and egotistical.

Sonja: And you lived with your grandmother?

Igor: Yes, as far as I can remember, the four of us always lived together. My father came to Krasnoyarsk after his army service and met my mother here. My grandmother, on my father's side, also came here and lived with us until the day she died.

Sonja: What did your parents do?

Igor: My mom worked as an economic planner in a radio-technical factory her whole life. She still works there now. That's an area of specialization we have in socialist society. I don't know what it would be in the West. My father was a welder in that same factory. It's very hard physical labor, and in the end he died at work. An aneurysm. For a time it was a munitions factory, and then it was declassified. Now it's being shut down completely. There's no demand for production.

Sonja: When did you first have feelings for members of your own sex?

Igor: My attraction to men happened very early, it was already completely conscious starting at the age of thirteen. I had sexual relations with classmates, and I never hid that, but I never went further than light petting. In school I assumed it was normal. I somehow thought that it was not at all unusual and that all people experienced sexual feelings for each other. It was only later, when I attended the medical institute and I began to study these things more deeply that I realized there were heterosexuals, homosexuals, and bisexuals. But up to the ages of seventeen or eighteen, I thought I was a completely normal and average person, like everyone.

Sonja: Did you talk to your parents about sex at home?

Igor: No, we never had any discussions about that topic, until the moment my parents found out I was a homosexual. I was twenty-one then. I didn't get any sex education, as it's called now.

Sonja: How did that happen? And how did they react?

Igor: Everything happened in a usual way. By that time I had already had many relationships. One day my mother discovered one of my love letters. She got a little upset and asked: "What is this!" I answered, "Well, it is what it is. That's how I am." Nothing else happened. As strange as it may seem, my parents took the news very calmly. Not that they took it for granted, but they agreed to see it as a done deal. Like something they couldn't change. That was in 1983. And after two years, when my father died, any problems that I'd had with my mother in that regard just disappeared. Now I don't hide anything; she knows who I am and who I'm with. Naturally, I don't go on about any intimate details, but everything else she knows and accepts easily.

Sonja: So you didn't feel excluded or alone in childhood or later?

Igor: It was at seventeen that I realized that I wasn't like everyone else. As far as loneliness, you know, it's not necessarily related to sexual orientation. Heterosexuals can be lonely, too. And you can be a homosexual and not suffer from it. By the way, in terms of sexual relations, sometimes I'm single, recently, for example. Probably because of my age.

Sonja: And what was going on with you when you were seventeen? What happened?

Igor: I felt true love for the first time. I was already studying at the Institute, so that means I wasn't seventeen, I was eighteen. A year after me, a young man entered the Institute. He was two years older than I was and we quickly became close. But that was all spiritual, platonic, no sexual relations, even touching, or even allusions to anything of the sort. Nonetheless, it was true love, my first love, and very enduring and constant. He didn't know the feelings that I had for him. And what's more, if you had told me that he knew about my feelings or that he might somehow return them, I would have run away.

That affected me very strongly. It was a real shock to my whole life. I can truly say that sex has never enticed me very much, not then and not later. For me, the feelings that I have for a person are far more important, even if they're just platonic.

Sonja: And what happened next?

Igor: As I said, I had strong feelings for him, but couldn't tell him about it. Maybe now in a similar situation I'd be able to explain. Then I didn't know what to do, but then all of the sudden it resolved itself. Some sort of medical commission discovered that he was seriously ill, that he had a heart problem. When they told him that, he was so upset that he decided to leave the Institute. He went to live in a different city. I followed him there in secret—he never knew. Now he lives in Sayanogorsk, in the Krasnoyarsk region. He's married and has children, two girls, I think. So my problems were solved. And after that I did everything. There were strictly sexual relationships, and some with serious feelings. Yeah, there was a lot.

Sonja: Where do gay people meet in Krasnoyarsk?

Igor: At one time we had places where gay people could meet each other. Should I list them? The square in front of the Opera and Ballet Theater, the Zlobino railroad station, the area in front of TsUM [the central department store]. Where else? The square in front of

North Airport. In summer, the resort island, there's Korstets Square. That's basically all of them. But that was before the eighties, when I was young. Then, in Russia, well, I think it was all over the world, the persecution of the gays started. When they arrested so many, all those [meeting places] ended. Now the old traditions are returning. As far as I know, you can find people at Zlobino Station, but most people make dates now through personal ads. In our region we have two newspapers, *Komok* and *Segodnyashnaya Gazeta,* which publish gay ads. They've been around since 1991. That's how people meet. They write and respond.

Sonja: Tell more about the times you were just recalling. What was this persecution and when?

Igor: It all started in 1983. I don't know what provoked it. As far as I know, trials under Article 121 [1934 anti-gay sex law instituted by Stalin] swept through Russia at that time, and throughout the Soviet Union. This law punished even voluntary homosexual relations. I don't know what the reason was for these trials. There were a lot of possibilities, starting with AIDS and ending with the rumor that the Women's Union of Russia had filed a grievance. In Krasnoyarsk this continued till 1986. As far as I know, we had six big trials, where 130 people were convicted. The most notorious was the last trial, when Anufriev was tried. He was the correspondent from the newspaper *Pionerskaya Pravda.* Then there were the 130 who were convicted, many more people were brought in to see the trials, even those who had escaped sentencing, including me. I wriggled out of it because they declared me insane.

Sonja: Really? How did that happen?

Igor: In the Regional Office of Internal Affairs, they created a special subdivision for the "struggle against sexual crimes." The employees, six or seven people, kept watching the places where homosexuals met and followed whoever went there. If they noticed that some person came repeatedly or stayed for an extended time, they showed him their identification and said, "Let's go." That's what happened to me.

At the police station they began exhaustive interrogations: "Do you know this one? Do you know that one? What do you think about such and such? What do you know?" Because of Article 121, they were counting on voluntary confessions. That's what they call it in criminal law. They said that if you "voluntarily confessed" that you've had sexual relations with men, they'd pardon you. As I understand it, all the trials of the 1980s were based on these types of voluntary confessions. No factual proof, no expert analysis existed. They took them to the station, sat them down and asked three or four people in a row: "What were you doing there?"

That's how it was in my case. I was cruising the square in front of the opera and ballet theater and I noticed three or four men who also seemed to be cruising. After half an hour, I started off for home and then one of the young men came up to me and said, "Excuse me, let's go." Where? "To the Central Office of the Ministry of Internal Affairs (RUVD)." Ok, just show me your identification. He showed me his lieutenant's ID. I said: "Ok, let's go." They invited me into to the RUVD and asked: "Do you know that homosexuals gather in these places?" "Yes I know. So what?" "How do you feel about that?" "How do you think I feel about it—I'm like that myself!" There was nothing more to ask.

Then they started showing me photo albums of criminals. I know that in these albums there were 2500 photographs of homosexuals, actually, of people who were suspected of having homosexual relations. I was certainly not the first. I was then asked to bring my own photograph. I brought the one I had made for my passport [when I was eighteen]. I was already twenty-five so they asked me to bring in a newer photo. I know that my name was mentioned in the second and third trials, but I never revealed who I had sexual contact with. Then

I was declared insane, thanks to the light-handed regional psychiatrist. In the end I did not go to trial.

Sonja: Why do you think they declared you insane?

Igor: When these trials started, I realized right away that since I knew a lot of people, they'd find me sooner or later. I didn't want to go to any prison, whatsoever; I knew what they did with people who were considered sexual minorities in correctional institutions. I didn't have to think twice before I declared that I was a homosexual and at the same time I provided my own defense. I went to the regional psychiatrist, who was a woman, and told her, "Well, look, I am that way. So what should I do?" They put me under observation for ten days in the psychiatric clinic and concluded that I was indeed homosexual. That's why, when the police asked me if I knew that gays met each other there, I bravely said that I was like that myself and added, "If you need anything else, please talk to my psychiatrist." They didn't bother me after that.

Sonja: So you had gone to see the psychiatrist in advance?

Igor: Yes, because I could see what was coming and I wanted to give myself a cover. As you can see, it worked.

Sonja: After that you didn't have any problems with the police?

Igor: No, never. Even with people who had tried at various points to get me arrested for homosexuality. When I set up my firm, I had some financial problems. Then I ran into a man who had worked with me on a gay matter. It turned out that he was now working for the department of "struggle against organized crime." I told him about my problems and he helped, although not really substantially. All the same, he tried to do something for me. I never had any more problems with the police.

Sonja: How did the doctors relate to you?

Igor: Very well. When it all started, I was still studying at the Institute and I went to our dean. I told him about what was going on, that they wanted to expel me from the Institute and maybe even arrest me. He sincerely wanted to help me and he suggested I speak to a psychiatrist. The next day I went to his office and the regional psychiatrist was there. She and I talked about everything and she said, "I understand you perfectly. I'll do everything necessary." Later I met with her many times, although I was already working at the television station. She and I continued to have an excellent relationship. I didn't have any problems with the dean, Valentin Lvovich, either. By the way, most people who I came into contact with at work, and in life, reacted very well when they found out that I was gay. There were never any negative feelings about me.

Sonja: Then, at the time of the trial, they declared you officially mentally ill. But you didn't actually think you were?

Igor: No, absolutely not. I never thought that I had any kind of psychological problem. I knew since I was eighteen. I knew that I had a different sexual orientation, not like most people, but I never felt I was abnormal.

Sonja: Was the psychiatrist's diagnosis attached to your documents?

Igor: Yes, to my military ID. In Russia, everything is related to military duty, and the relevant data is in my military ID. See, there's the stamp.

Sonja: What does it say?

Igor: That the military-medical commission found me unfit for service according to statute 7B. Statute 7B means "psychopathology with no physiological basis." So I am officially considered a psychopath for the rest of my life. That certificate will not be reevaluated ever again. But really it doesn't hurt me in any way.

Sonja: Do you need to show that document to apply for a job?

Igor: It used to be required for some high-risk jobs. Drivers, pilots. But it doesn't cause any problems for other work.

Sonja: How did you end up being expelled from school?

Igor: As I said before, everyone I knew protected me and even the leadership of the department was on my side. The dean, teachers, students, everyone except the rector. That's who destroyed me. When I told the dean about everything and that they wanted to take me to court and so on, he, naturally, had to tell the rector about this complex situation. The rector told him: you figure out what to do, but don't mix me up in that situation. The dean offered to let me go on academic leave, a kind of a temporary unpaid leave of absence. I had to discuss the continuation of my studies with the rector himself. The rector said: "I have nothing to talk to you about." And for all intents and purposes he forced me to leave the Institute forever. As a result, I never finished college.

I still can't forgive the rector, even though he's dead. I met him many years later, on business for my firm. When I arrived, he didn't recognize me right away, and he said, "We've met somewhere before." I answered: "Of course we met in '83 when you threw me out of the Institute" "For what?" "For homosexuality." You should have seen his reaction. Of course he didn't let on, but our interaction suddenly got cold as ice. That's what happened.

Sonja: And where did you work next? How did people act towards you at work?

Igor: After the Institute, when I supposedly went on academic leave, I went to work in the television station. I worked there for five years or so, as a director. The first year nobody knew I was gay, I never advertised it. But when they did find out, they were completely fine with it. There was only one exception. The gay trials were still going on. One of our other directors, in order to curry favor, wrote up a complaint about me and that I was associating with a person who was accused of criminal acts. But it backfired. They dragged him off as a witness, and they already knew all about me. Since I had been declared insane, they couldn't touch me. That director suddenly began to speak so well of me that I was amazed. The rest were all wonderful to me from the start.

Sonja: What's your living situation? Do you have a partner?

Igor: Right now? For more than six months I haven't had anyone. In general, I'd like to have a partner, not be with one person today and another tomorrow and a third one the next day. Unfortunately, I have a very eccentric personality and it's hard for me to live with people. I don't often have a partner, and when I do, I start arguing right away.

Sonja: Who do you socialize with? Only with gay men or with other people, too?

Igor: I have a very wide social circle. Gay, hetero, and bisexual. I have two very good female friends. Really, at first there was one, and now there's another. They are very heterosexual. But both of them know all about me and relate very well to me. In Russia, the word for female friend [*podruga*] often means lover, but in this case I really mean female friends. We have such a good relationship that we can sit down with a cup of coffee and gossip about our sexual problems. She tells me about hers and I tell her about mine, until we come to a mutual understanding. I also know some men, you could even call them good friends, who are heterosexual. They know I'm gay and it doesn't bother them. Of course I know a lot of gay men, but few of them are real friends. There are gay men who I would prefer never to see again.

Sonja: I heard that you tried to establish a gay organization in town?

Igor: Yes, in 1990, when they still hadn't repealed Article 121. My acquaintances helped me distribute the necessary information. Then, the most important task was to get people to meet one another, bring them together. We took care of that. I don't do that work anymore, but as far as I know, all the people who met through the service SASM (Siberian Association of Sexual Minorities) are continuing to meet. This is the data from the current year and the end of last year. The goal of the association was achieved. What I aimed for is still working out well. One can say that I didn't just try, but I really did establish that organization. By the way, it was one of the first gay organizations in the USSR. The first was in Moscow, which was started by Kalinin [*Tema*]. Then there was one in St. Petersburg, I don't even remember who was in charge of that one. And the third organization was ours. In Russia proper, anyway. I don't have information about the other republics of the former Soviet Union. Then they started organizing in Barnaul, in Novosibirsk, Khabarovsk. But we were the third in Russia, so I think I did do something good.

Sonja: How do gay people refer to themselves in Russia?

Igor: I don't know what they do now, but in my youth we used nicknames, usually feminine. Sometimes they reflected the character or the appearance of the person, sometimes they were just random. If a nickname stuck, that's what he was called going forward. Even now we do that. First and last names are all the same, but a nickname really brings out individuality.

Sonja: For example?

Igor: Well, for example, when I was seventeen, and when I first showed up in the gay community, they called me Chinny [in feminine gender], because my chin stuck out. Then, once I started feeling at home with it, they gave me the pompous name of Dowager Queen Mother Chinny Anna on the Neck [referring to Chekhov's story]. Why? Just to have fun. Much more interesting. Of course, nobody called me that long name in conversation. Usually it turned into Anna or sometimes Baba Anya. It was all the same to me. Most of the time when people talked about someone in the third person, they used a nickname. Sometimes they just said: girl, girlfriend, or darling, all in feminine gender. Some, of course, are offended by this.

Sonja: When did the terms *goluboy* [blue] and *gay* first appear?

Igor: When did they start? Sometime in the 1980s. I learned those words in '85 or '86 during *perestroika*. But mostly we used the ones I mentioned. I've known them practically since I was a kid.

Sonja: The gay community has a negative attitude toward prison slang, right?

Igor: Yes.

Sonja: Do you also?

Igor: It's completely unacceptable. I don't even want to say it. There's a slang word, "rooster." It's a slur not only in our circles, but everywhere. Even worse is the most vulgar word, *pederast*, which comes from the Greek *paiderastes*. That word is used only when you really want to put someone down, even if that the person does not belong to a sexual minority.

Sonja: Did you ever have sexual relations with a woman?

Igor: No, absolutely not. Never, not once. I didn't want to. And I hope I never will. Not at all.

Sonja: Have you ever known any celebrities or politicians who were publicly gay? For example, did you know that Tchaikovsky was gay?

Igor: In my time, no.

Sonja: When did you first hear about it?

Igor: About Tchaikovsky? The late 1980s. And before then I didn't suspect it at all. I might think that about our singer Leontiev. He became famous sometime in 1975 and I felt right away that he was the same as me. I found out about the others a little later.

Sonja: And what about writers or professionals?

Igor: I was never really interested in them. Really, I've always said that before 1980 I thought everyone was like that. It was only when the trials started that there were problems. From the end of 1982 to 1985 I was as quiet as a mouse. A mouse is so little; she sneaks into a corner and just hides. After 1985, by the time they brought up the question of whether to repeal Article 121, I really didn't care.

Sonja: Has anything changed for gay people since the Soviet era?

Igor: Now there's no law in the criminal code. Basically, that's the only change. It's important. I wouldn't want that law applied to me or to anyone else. I hope that those trials won't happen again, but there is no guarantee. Otherwise there's no difference. Society relates to us just as negatively as before. At least the young people now have better information, and some sort of gay movement has appeared.

Sonja: In general, don't you think life has changed?

Igor: That's a difficult question. Honestly? It's gotten harder for me to survive. In the past, a TV director's salary of 110 rubles would allow me to vacation for a whole month in Kiev. Now that's impossible. One of my friends went on vacation to Yalta recently. It's also the Ukraine, and he had to pay five million rubles, or about one thousand dollars. In Russia, vacations are even more expensive. If he had gone to Sochi he would have had to spend ten million.

Sonja: Do you want to add anything?

Igor: I think I answered all your questions, Sonja. I suppose that's enough.

Misha

Interviewed in 1995

Translated by Sonja Franeta

Born in Krasnodar in 1960, Misha was an anesthesiologist in the Novosibirsk Regional Hospital when I interviewed him. He told me he didn't want to hide his sexual orientation anymore, even if he was threatened or harassed. Like the majority of gay men, he was in hiding all his life, and now, with the chance to be himself, he has no desire to return to his past way of life.

Sonja: Misha, where you were born? What did your parents do for a living?

Misha: My father was born in 1934 into a family of Volga peasants. At the time, the fate of those peasants was horrible. They were deprived of all their rights as citizens. They had no passports. They could not change their place of residence. They could leave their villages in only two ways. Youth could join the local military training center. Women could get married to city dwellers. Those were the only two ways they could leave. There was no other way out.

My father got into a military training school. After he finished, he spent twenty-five years in the army as an officer—first, in the Russian Far East on the Kuril Islands. In 1959, when Khrushchev declared the formation of rocket stations in the USSR, my father passed his qualifying exams for rocket military officer and was sent to serve in the western part of the country—all the way in Kaliningrad, a former territory of Eastern Prussia.

I was my parents' first child. When my mother was pregnant with me, she went to her family in Armavir, in the Krasnodar region, where I was born. I spent my whole childhood there. In 1977, I finished secondary school with honors and began attending the First Medical Institute in Leningrad. I completed the necessary courses at the Institute, and in 1983, I became a doctor. Two years later I received a specialty in anesthesiology and resuscitation. It's been twelve years, and since then, I have worked in my specialty.

When I was still at the Institute, my father finished his military service. He went into retirement and our family moved here, to Novosibirsk. My parents convinced me to move with them also. I've lived in Novosibirsk since 1987 and have worked as an anesthesiologist and physician.

Sonja: Why did they decide to move to Novosibirsk?

Misha: My younger sister and brother were grown up; they are twins. My parents wanted them to have higher education. My mother really didn't like it that I went to college in a different city, far from the family. She wanted the younger children to have higher education but be near them. Her father had lived in Novosibirsk for many years and she decided it would be better to settle here.

Sonja: Are your parents Russian?

Misha: My father is Russian. My mother's father was Ukrainian but her mother was Polish. I am a mixture of three Slavic ethnicities: Russian, Ukrainian, and Polish. From the beginning of *perestroika,* religious freedom in the USSR became a reality. I was baptized in the Catholic faith, like my mother's relatives. Within myself I feel more Polish than Russian.

Sonja: Why is that?

Misha: It's hard to explain; it's some kind of intuitive feeling. Looking at the relatives on my father's side and my mother's, I feel that the best parts of me have come from my Polish ancestors.

Sonja: When you were small, did your mother work?

Misha: In the Soviet Union, both parents were supposed to work to support the family. My mother was educated as a professional economist. She worked all her life.

Sonja: Did you grow up in a Catholic family?

Misha: No, we were atheists. Only later when I was twenty-seven years old did I choose the Catholic Church.

Sonja: Did your family talk about politics?

Misha: We never had any dissident-like conversations. My father was an officer in the Soviet army and they all had to be members of the Communist Party. Any form of disloyalty was strictly punished. My parents were loyal to the Communist regime. I grew up in those conditions. I never crossed paths with any person who had opposite views, throughout my childhood.

The first time I thought that something was not right with our government's ideal kingdom was when I started at the Institute. In Leningrad, now St. Petersburg once again, I ended up in an intellectual circle where dissident conversations took place. I began to understand that the Communist reality and its ideology were terrible deceptions. But in my childhood I truly believed in communist ideals and I was ready to swear allegiance to Communism.

Sonja: When did you first have feelings for those of the same-sex?

Misha: This happened very early. I could say with absolute certainty that when I was five years old, when I was going to kindergarten, I already knew that I liked boys more than girls. Children often play sexual games. I paid attention to the fact that it was more interesting for me to play these games with boys. In the beginning this didn't seem dangerous, even though I asked myself from time to time, was this okay, should it be this way. I first seriously thought about it when I was fourteen or fifteen. I did not even know the word homosexuality, and I was pretty shocked. Becoming conscious of myself as different from everyone else was scary. Furthermore, the USSR official medical world did not include sexuality. That theme was forbidden. Even minimal, trustworthy knowledge of this subject was impossible to obtain. In the end, Soviet psychiatry concluded that homosexuality was a pathology, a psychological illness.

When I came across this, I became very afraid. My primary thought was that someone could find out about my homosexuality. I experienced terrible misgivings. I started having insomnia and terrible nightmares. Especially, living in a small provincial town, where a homosexual is almost always alone with his problems. You cannot find anyone with a good attitude or viewpoint, especially in an environment of fear and ideological oppression.

Sonja: But had you heard that there were people like you?

Misha: No, while I lived with my family I had no idea that they existed. At the time I was truly convinced that I was the only one like that. To be conscious of this was awful. If in kindergarten, our sexual games were not under our conscious control and more or less spontaneous, during the period of sexual maturing, one begins to wonder about the right to be who he wants to be. Maybe there were such people as me in my immediate surroundings but I simply was not aware. They probably also lived with the same fear.

When I was fifteen, I started technical school and studied there for a year. I lived separately from my family. In the center of town there was a park where gays gathered. I actually did not know anything about what they did but I liked going there. It was a very comfortable place: a shady park with benches. You could rest, sit, read. Here is where I first learned that men could be interested in me. A few very actively went after me. I was still an adolescent. When men tried to get to know me and show what they expected of me, I got scared. One time, curiosity won over my fear. My first sexual contact with an adult man took place in 1975, in Kaliningrad.

It was then that I had real sex with an adult man. That first contact was very good for me. There was a feeling of distaste that remained with me though and it took me a long time to repeat this experience. But all my erotic fantasies were relentless and involved men. In the meeting places, I was always drawn to men who were attractive to me erotically.

Sonja: When you were a child, did the other kids tease you because you were not like the rest?

Misha: No, never. All childhood sexual games were by mutual agreement. The interest was mutual.

Sonja: At what point did you understand what you were feeling?

Misha: It was a big internal conflict for me. For a few years I tried to bury my sexuality in a dark corner of my soul. I thought of it as a bad habit. I thought if I could only work on it, if I could concentrate my will, then I could get rid of it. Honestly, I was convinced of this. The first time in my life I told myself I had the right to be myself, I was only twenty-eight.

Sonja: How did that happen?

Misha: At that point I got access to research information on the nature of human sexuality for the first time. It was already *perestroika*. The books that had been hidden away and forbidden to be read became accessible. They started to re-issue studies by Russian medical people who had written on this theme before October of 1917. They also started to publish research work by foreign authors in Russian. When I got access to this information and comprehended it all, I came to the conclusion that this was in my nature. I was born this way and I had the right to be the way I am. After this, the problem was finding people like me, so it would be easier for me psychologically. I needed them not so much for sex, as to be myself within a circle of friends. This happen to me at the age of twenty-eight. Before that, I was completely stressed out, especially when I found out that the laws of the USSR included an anti-gay law, and that you could go to prison for it.

Sonja: Did you ever have any dealings with the authorities on this question?

Misha: No, I never had those problems. I was always very careful. Even if I went somewhere for sexual contact with a man, I would choose a partner who could be reliable and could guarantee anonymity for me.

Sonja: How did you meet your partners? Did you go to meeting places?

Misha: I knew where the places were, but I never went inside them. I watched from the sidelines. I observed those people who frequented them and also how they conducted themselves, and I picked men out. "With that man I would probably like to have sex," I thought. Then when he left the place, I would go after him. When he got onto a bus or a streetcar, I would sit near him in one of those means of transportation, which was usually packed with passengers. I'd demonstrate my sexual interest, easily. Seizing the moment, I would pass my hand over an appropriate part of his body—and that was it. A dialogue would strike up. To that young man, I was very good-looking. I was actually quite popular among gay men. Therefore, if I decided to show interest in someone, I was absolutely sure there wouldn't be a rejection.

These sexual contacts were episodic. There were no long-term relationships. Furthermore, my sexual partners did not show interest in anything like that. These episodic contacts guaranteed anonymity. It was possible to spend time with a person and not even find out his name, and then part with him forever. In those years I could say with complete certainty that there were practically no long-term relationships among gays. People were concerned with whether everything could be kept secret.

Sonja: But did you fall in love?

Misha: Yes, more than once. Sexuality, for me, is strongly connected with my emotional self. When I grew up, I understood sex could only bring me deeper satisfaction with the man I loved.

When I was twenty to twenty-two years old, I had many one-night stands. Of course I had sex not only with those who I was sexually attracted to, but it was also emotional. I saw that I could either fall in love with a person or want to fall in love with a person. From that age I started to make some brave attempts indicating to my partners that I wanted some continuation of relations. But as a rule they did not take me up on this. They were afraid of long-term relationships.

It turned out that I did not have sex with those I fell madly in love with. I had long-term friendships with men and I experienced sexual attraction with them. But out of fear of shocking them or scaring them away, I had to hide my love. All this led to periods of depression on my part. From my friends' point of view, I lacked motivation. It became hard for them to socialize with me, because I could not tell them the truth. Finally, it all ended in a break in relations. From this I suffered greatly. This happened more than once.

Sonja: Can you tell me about these cases in more detail?

Misha: When I was studying at the Institute, I was in love with a classmate. We were friends for five years. For him, as well as for those around us, it was a friendship between two guys. No one even suspected I was in love with him. Because of the impossibility of sexual contact with him, I sought something in return. I constantly needed from him some kind of proof of friendship. If I did not get this, I fell into depression. Sometimes the situation led to actual hysteria. From the friend's point of view, this was completely incomprehensible. When an argument ended, it was necessary to make peace, to invent reasons for my behavior and then naturally I had to lie. I did not see any possibility of telling him the truth.

The most tormenting moments were when we went to the baths. I saw him without his clothes on. I was terribly attracted to him. But I understood that I could never touch him to get some release. This gave me terrible physical suffering. At the time he and I lived in a communal household. Students, as is well-known, are very unassuming in their household duties. They make peace with their discomforts. Very often when there were a lot of people, we all slept together in one bed. I also sometimes slept with my friend under one blanket. For me this was a big trial. I could not hug him, could not kiss him, could not caress him. I was afraid to scare him off. After those nights I would wake up in the morning in a terrible depression. My bad mood was incomprehensible to him. Finally, he began to see me as a person with an unstable psyche and unpredictable behavior. It became difficult for him to socialize with me. Thank God, I was courageous enough to be the first to end our friendship. Because the initiative for the break came from me, it gave me some sort of moral satisfaction. I ended it quite demonstratively, although it tortured me.

I needed something to help me forget my failure in the erotic sphere. By nature, I am an intense person with a strong artistic sensitivity. Good serious literature and art have distracted me from my worries connected with sex. Also, of course, masturbation helped me, during which I could use my entire arsenal of erotic fantasies. This was not some kind of primitive surrogate, I received real satisfaction and peace for a period of time.

Sonja: Did your parents know about your orientation?

Misha: No, my parents, my family, did not know anything then. My mother found out about this from me only three years ago. This happened, by the way, after our first conversation at that time. After thinking about it, I decided to reveal myself to my mother. Right after your [Sonja's] departure from Novosibirsk last time, I told my mother everything.

Sonja: How did your mom react to this?

Misha: At first of course she was a bit shocked. She knew very little about the realm of sex. She very quickly collected herself and said something completely wonderful: "Well, I gave birth to you and that's who you are!" I was very thankful to her and I consider this a fine reaction. We talked about it and decided not to say anything to my father. He could hardly be expected to understand me and it was not worth embarrassing him. My brother also didn't know anything, nor did my sister. Well, I think she sort of guessed. I didn't say anything to her, but she's a doctor and she know things about human sexuality. Observing me and my way of life, she probably has come to some conclusions. But she has never said anything to me. Obviously she thinks I have a right to my personal life and doesn't want to interfere. I am very thankful to her for this.

Sonja: Do you live with your parents?

Misha: No, I have a separate apartment. When I figured out that I was gay, I decided that I had to live separately from my family. I had to take care of the psyches of my people. There was no reason to continuously remind them of my homosexuality.

Sonja: Did your sexual orientation affect your choice of profession?

Misha: No, my sexual orientation had nothing to do with it. At first I tried technical school. I studied for about a year but I realized it was not interesting to me. I liked the humanitarian sciences more and also foreign languages. But at that time in the USSR, all the humanitarian sciences were ideological. To do that work meant working hand in hand with the regime's leadership. That didn't feel right to me. Learning foreign languages was interesting but that didn't offer me much hope or a prospective profession. At that time we lived in certain closed conditions behind the Iron Curtain and there was no practical reason in knowing languages. In the end I chose a profession that was a cross between humanitarian and natural sciences—medicine. I knew that when I became a doctor I could really help people.

Sonja: Did you have problems at work because you were gay?

Misha: At first, yes. In those years the KGB showed a great interest in homosexuals. They actually had plans to devote an entire department to this. We were under KGB surveillance and they had files on people. I was not an exception, the authorities showed a concerted interest in me. They sent around requests for references from colleagues at work and they asked questions about me. There were no traitors among them, thank God. My colleagues did not give the KGB the information they needed. But all this was very unpleasant. While indirectly they indicated that they knew a thing or two about me, behind my back there were rumors. Naturally I was alarmed at this. After not getting information from my colleagues, the KGB began to follow me. I myself saw people tracking me, and they tried to control my personal life.

Sonja: When did all this happen?

Misha: At first, it was during my medical career in Kaliningrad, where I first went to work upon finishing the Institute. By the time I moved to Novosibirsk in 1987, there were no more problems with the KGB. The situation in the country had radically changed. There are still problems to this day but they are completely different. I don't have any insecurities being gay. Now I'm not afraid that someone would find out about it. I can talk freely about it, even with heterosexuals.

I became open with almost everyone I loved and respected. I told my friends and acquaintances, whoever I thought necessary. I must say they all related to it completely okay. Still I don't have someone who I can really call my beloved. For me this is a real source of anguish. Here, in Novosibirsk, I know about two hundred or more gays. Out of these two hundred, there is not one who is a match for me. For some time I have known that sex without love is not for me. I don't go for one night stands. I prefer not to have sex at all than to waste my time on one-time satisfactions. It is possible that I will have to wait for my love for a long time. Maybe, all my life. But I am not discouraged and I believe it will come. I will never kill myself, which my boyfriend did two months ago.

Sonja: What happened?

Misha: He was twenty-seven and he was an accountant. He was in love with me. I could not return the feeling, although I related to him quite well. Love is complicated. Maybe I even tried to fall in love with him but I couldn't. I tried not to hurt his feelings. When he wanted sex he got it, but there was no love. You can't fool a person.

He was a poet at heart, but he could not express himself. I guess he felt that nobody understood him. He couldn't put up with his conflicted existence. Nobody got it that he was in crisis. He lived with his mother and even she did not pick up on this. She went to see her neighbors for twenty minutes and in those twenty minutes he had managed to hang himself in the bathroom. We buried him on April 10. For me it is a terrible grief and to this day I cannot come out of a terrible depression. I try not to show this to people, but it is so difficult for me. I started to look at many things differently. Everything else seems pitiful, insignificant, and useless, compared to the loss of this one good man's life.

Sonja: I'm sorry. (Pause)

Have you ever had relationships with women?

Misha: This question I cannot answer simply and directly. No, I did not have sex with even one woman. Never. I always felt intuitively that this would not give me anything, only disappointment. That would be an ugly lie on my part. I'm actually proud of the fact that I didn't feel it necessary to experiment with women. I didn't even make an attempt to have a heterosexual marriage in order to gain a positive opinion among people. By the way, I knew guys who did get married. They lived a double life, in constant fear that they would be found out by their wives. Russian women are very proprietary. If a woman finds out that her husband is a homosexual, she would regard this as an infringement on her lawful rights. Her reaction would be awful and the consequences for her husband could be catastrophic.

Sonja: Did you know about Tchaikovsky's homosexuality in your younger years? Were you aware of other people in literature and the arts who were gay?

Misha: No, literature and the arts were under the watchful eye of the censor. All information of that kind was blotted out. Only at the beginning of *perestroika* was it even possible to talk about this publicly. That's why I just recently found out about Oscar Wilde, Michelangelo, Leonardo da Vinci, and Tchaikovsky, only ten years ago. But I was very happy. These are the people who are the pride of humanity. They had a great influence on history, civilization, and culture.

Sonja: What words did you use early on when you talked about homosexuality?

Misha: I was always shocked by the word *pederast*. Also, I never used legal words. If someone began using these words, I would leave the conversation. Of course the word *pedik*, the diminutive for *pederast,* is a word I have sometimes used, but only in conversations with our people [queers].

Also, in Soviet times the term *goluboy* [blue, the word for gay] became widespread. I heard it in my student years. I always liked the term. It had a kind of romantic aura. The blue of the sky and my homosexuality—that association was very pleasant for me. I use that word most of the time.

Sonja: Do you know where it came from?

Misha: I don't know what the origin is. I don't think anyone really knows where it came from, But I have a theory. I think it arose with the bohemian artistic social set at the beginning of this century, among artists, painters, and musicians. It was called the Silver Age of Russian culture. At that time there was a very tolerant attitude towards homosexuality, probably the best time in all of Russian history. Of course, it's only a theory.

Sonja: Why do you think they related well to gays at that time?

Misha: It's well-known from literature. Actors, artists, poets openly demonstrated their homosexuality. The most famous one at the time was the poet Kuzmin. On Mars Field in St. Petersburg there was a famous cabaret called *The Stray Dog*. All the bohemians got together there. Homosexuality was not only open there, it was nurtured there.

Sonja: Can you make a comparison between Soviet times and the current times? Has anything changed?

Misha: For us, the main accomplishment has been changes in the criminal code, the repeal of the article against gay sex. That has given so many people the ability to come out of the closet. Not only to talk openly about one's sexuality, but at least not to feel that panic and fear. Learning to live in harmony with oneself. Many have said to themselves: if I am that way, I am no longer a criminal. I have a right to a personal life. That right has been conclusively confirmed by the new Russian Constitution.

The greatest dream for every homosexual is the right to be himself and to talk about himself openly in any society. Russia is still far from this. Mass psychology changes very slowly. Much can be repealed with the mark of a pen, but relationships among people are a different thing. That's a long process. We may not be afraid of our homosexuality, but not all people in our circles are able to understand us properly. We still have to exercise some caution. This is not fear, there's no more fear, but the problems in society remain. I know that I and others agree.

Sonja: But in general is life better now?

Misha: Life has not become better. New problems have arisen, they're economic. In earlier days they tried to inspire us with, "Work! Don't worry! We are taking care of you; we will give you everything you need for your lives." People thought: "I will earn a living for a number of hours and the government will grant me an apartment, paid leave, paid vacation time, even time at a resort." Now this patriarchal caretaking has disappeared. One fine day we realized that no one owed us anything. We knew that we ourselves had to take care of ourselves. We had to change our thinking and that wasn't easy, especially with the onset of an economic crisis.

There's also one more serious psychological phenomenon. The government has announced officially that we are on the road to restoring capitalism, on the path to privatization. The former party economic apparatus has taken over almost all enterprises owned by the people. The majority of the population believed that everyone would receive what is owed them. That would have been fair. But now people feel tricked and this is well-founded. The government has tricked them once again, abandoned them to their fates. This brings up for most people a profound dissatisfaction with life—aggression and anger. People are ready to consider anyone a personal enemy. It's very difficult to live under those kinds of conditions.

In earlier times, the official propaganda created the image of an external enemy in the form of the USA. Now it is funny to remember this. I grew up with the conviction that America was a bad thing, that America was horrible, that good people could never live there. But the image of an internal enemy was also developed. Someone else had to be responsible for our problems, not we ourselves. Many still live in such an environment. They look for the guilty party. Anyone could fit the role of the enemy, including gays. "You're bothering me! Oh, and you're also gay? I'll let you have it!"

We live in the real world and we have to take everything into account. We may not have the earlier kind of fear, but we have to be careful to control our behavior. You can only be yourself in your own circle where we try to create a kind of micro-society to feel comfortable and cozy. But outside of these boundaries you have to be careful and circumspect as before.

Russia is a country of political instability. We don't know who will show up in the role of a leader on any given day. This could be someone who would again start poisoning homosexuals. This turn of events could actually happen. We live one day at a time. We try not to think about what will be tomorrow. But I am ready to announce with full responsibility that I will not change my convictions. Even if my life were threatened with real danger, even if they start sending people to Kolyma, the gulag, this doesn't scare me. I won't betray others to save my own life. I could swear this on the Bible.

My biggest and most passionate desire is to find love. I cannot imagine life without it. I live with the feeling that it will come to me imminently. This gives me the strength to overcome difficulties and it inspires hope in me.

Sergey

Interviewed in 1995
Translated by Lara Ravitch
Edited by Sonja Franeta

Sergey was born in Tomsk in 1951. Animated and friendly, he has a medium build. When he smiles, he has pronounced dimples. He is leader of the organization Astarte, officially registered in Tomsk—an organization that supports sexual minorities and advocates for their rights. He worked with city government officials to prepare for the Pink Flamingo Film Festival in 1996. It was a success and brought a lot of publicity to Tomsk for the cause of LGBTQ rights.

Sonja: Tell me a little about your childhood and family.

Sergey: I was born in 1951, in Tomsk. My mother and father later told me they had been in a prison colony, so I was born in the prison camp. According to the law, my mother was released a short while after my birth. They released her under the 101 Kilometer rule but this meant that she couldn't live in a big city. She went to the northern part of Tomsk Region, to a village only reachable by airplane or by crossing the water. That's where my grandpa lived, a *kulak* [prosperous farmer] in exile. I spent some time there. After that Mama was able to move us three children to Tomsk. After they took away some of the limitations on her residency, she registered there and found work. Mama separated from my father who stayed in the village. She raised us alone. From fourth to eighth grade I studied at a state boarding school and then I went to work. I worked a little, while I was studying at the Tomsk regional music school. I finished technical high school with a major in radio communication and broadcasting. I worked at a factory and then for a while at the Palace of Culture, where I was in sound design. Now I'm working again in my field of specialty. That's it.

Sonja: Why was your grandfather sent to the North?

Sergey: My grandpa on my father's side had lived in the Altai Mountains before. He had a big family, a lot of land and livestock. The farm was doing well, the harvests were plentiful. Naturally, when the campaign to get rid of the *kulaks* started, they couldn't leave him alone. The Soviet leadership didn't like that sort of farmer, and so they exiled him to the northern part of Tomsk region. It was done on a massive scale in the Soviet Union. People were herded onto barges and floated down the Ob River. It was a completely uninhabited region. To survive there it was necessary to plow the soil and grow something. The exiles settled and winter caught up with them. They made sod dugouts and tried to live with whatever they had with them—tools, anything they had. Many couldn't hold out and died. My grandfather, grandmother and father were able to survive under those conditions. So that's how we ended up there.

I remember my grandfather perfectly; I've been told that I look like him. Without his beard, I really do look a lot like him. I'm just as intrusive and pushy. I remember one curious episode. I went to visit him in the country. He took me by the hand and said, "Come along, Sergey, let's go to the river." We went to the river. He said, "Get undressed." I asked, "What do you mean? All the way?" He said, "All the way." I got undressed. He said, "Swim." I swam, and when I got out, he gave me the towel and said: "It's as if it was me who went swimming." That really touched me. I didn't realize he could sense me so well.

Sonja: Is your nationality Russian?

Sergey: Yes, Russian. My grandpa and grandma on my mother's side came to Siberia from Vyatka in Central Russia during the Stolypin Reforms [when over ten million people were resettled to Siberia under tsarism]. They lived in Tomsk ever since.

Sonja: Did your family practice any kind of religion?

Sergey: Both of my grandmothers were religious, Russian Orthodox. Soon after I was born, they baptized me, secretly, since the government didn't allow it, so I'm Orthodox.

Sonja: Where did you live when you came to town?

Sergey: At my grandmother's, nine people in a twelve-meter room. Later we were somehow able to get an apartment.

Sonja: Who's the oldest in your family?

Sergey: I'm the youngest. I have a brother, Yura. My older brother, Gena, is already dead.

Sonja: Tell me a little about your work.

Sergey: I worked in the Palace of Culture. My responsibilities included running large cultural events. I love that work. I like to work with people. Sometimes I was the Master of Ceremony at concerts. I even recited poetry on stage. I love to read poetry by Esenin and Blok. In general, I like lyric poetry a lot.

The Palace of Culture belonged to the military department, which left its particular stamp on it. I had to give a statement swearing secrecy because there were often Party meetings, production discussions, and even discussions of military secrets. I didn't know anything about them, but I served at these events. I signed the pledge and it was difficult for me. There were strict controls, very strict controls.

At one time I was even secretary of the primary Komsomol organization. I did that just as a formality, to have some possibility of promotion. At that time, if you weren't a Komsomol member or a Communist, it was impossible to make anything of your life. But I didn't join the Party.

Sonja: How did they treat you at work? Did people know you were gay?

Sergey: When I ran the dance club, I worked with many different people. They noticed I didn't socialize much with women. There were rumors, speculation: "He's probably that way." But it never went beyond rumors. Nobody had any issues with my work. Nobody asked openly about my orientation. They could have used it against me, talked behind my back, and given me a certain reputation. Naturally that would have affected my work, my career. For example, I took part in the building of the Palace of Culture and did the sound and lighting design. I'm proud I could do that. If I had admitted that I was gay at the time, they wouldn't have let me near it.

Here we don't do things up front, but behind closed doors, on the sly. Why did you get fired? They just let you go. We have a song "They don't lock you up like Mandela, they just lay you off." At work I was always uncomfortable. They treated me, so to speak, like a trash can: we probably should throw it out but we might need it for something in the house. That's the kind of job I have. It's hard to find people in my area of expertise, so they need me. That's why they put up with me.

Sonja: Did you have to keep quiet?

Sergey: Before, I couldn't talk about it at all. If I had said anything, I would have lost my job, and maybe even gotten arrested. At the beginning of the 80s they tried to bring me up on criminal charges, send me to jail, not on Article 121 [which criminalizes homosexuality] but on another charge. As a rule, they used other laws when there wasn't clear evidence. I wasn't around minors, didn't force anyone to be with me. I only had consensual encounters. I was respectful, loved the person, got along with him. Therefore, it was very hard to get me on the gay law, to find witnesses for court. They looked for other ways, maybe some kind of violation at work. In Russia we say, "You can interpret the law however you want."

Sonja: And now how do people act towards you now?

Sergey: In society, gay people are treated like bums, homeless people. Basically they think that being gay and being a beggar are the same thing. It's considered low-life, dirty, vulgar, stupid, and that it is caused by laziness, perversion, bad upbringing, or whatever else they say. You always have to prove you're a person, just like everyone else. I have a friend, Sergey who is a poet, a bard. He plays guitar and sings, a very interesting person. One day we were sitting here with the group, drinking, and at one point, when we were both in the kitchen, I told him I was gay. He went back to the room, poured a glass of vodka, and said to my brother, "Yura, listen, we have to get Sergey some treatment." My brother, who has known about me for a long time, looked at him and said, "For what?" Then this friend told me I should not call him at work. It went on like that for about a month. Then he got interested: What? How? Why? Where does it come from? Does it happen to children? Do I go after children? He never knew anything about me for years.

Sonja: What words do you use when you talk about yourself to others?

Sergey: It depends on the situation, on who I'm talking to. I take into account the maturity level of the person. I can use many words.

Sonja: For example?

Sergey: *Goluboy*, [blue=gay] *or pedik*. I always know what to say but first, I have to prove myself as a person, that I can work, that I'm the same as them. It's only later that I can say I am gay. It shocks people at first, and then they get interested. They start to ask about it: How can you like men? How do you have a relationship? How do you screw? Supposedly, they're interested in the act itself. I tell them loving someone doesn't only mean screwing. I try to explain, but people have trouble understanding. And this is in Tomsk, a pretty big city, where we have Astarte, a gay and lesbian association. Just imagine a person living in the North, in the countryside, let's say, working as a teacher. He has to get married and have children. How would he feel? He could never come out, because everyone would point at him. He would either have to move away or hang himself.

The public is completely uninformed and misinformed. In the three years that Astarte has been around, I have not once been able to get an interview with the media, not on TV, not on the radio. Even if they did an interview, they'd never show it. Very recently, when we had a conference, I gave an interview, too. They promised to air it, but, again, they never did. All around us is a conspiracy of silence—"We don't have *that* here. *That* doesn't exist." And if they do say something, it's always negative. They make fun of us. Here is a typical example. There was a live televised broadcast of a regional festival and the announcer said on the air, "Everyone is gathered here today on the square. The whole town of Tomsk, the regional representatives, even the gays made an appearance." You see the word *even*. They constantly emphasize it like we crawled out from under a rock or something, from the margins of life, black sheep. It's sad. Even now it's very hard to come out. Maybe in Moscow or other big cities there are people who can speak out openly, but here, no.

I feel uncomfortable in my own town. Until recently, even the newspaper *AIDS-Info* was sold wrapped in a brown packet. The city government said that selling such literature wasn't allowed, even if it was educational. We don't have programs about this issue on TV, on the radio, or in any other media. If any comments are made, they are sarcastic. It's a vacuum. They don't talk about it in schools, or anywhere. It's all hidden, a complete vacuum. Isn't Siberia just a big prison?.

Sonja: Have you ever had any run-ins with criminals?

Sergey: Yes, I get robbed regularly, every year. The last time was in May. They took my radio, money, and other things worth a lot of money. I went to the police every time, but they didn't find anything. The police don't want to protect us. OK, so they robbed you, why are you making such a big deal about it? Be like everyone else and everything will be fine. I've already had a lot of run-ins with the district office because of this and with the police department. They don't want to hear anything, when you speak openly. They're afraid.

Sonja: And did your family speak openly about sexual issues?

Sergey: No, that issue was absolutely closed. The same with school. They never explained anything to us. We had to figure out everything ourselves. That was hard.

Sonja: And how did your mother react?

Sergey: I was her last child, her favorite. She didn't understand me but loved me very much. She lived a difficult life and raised three children. She didn't have time for judgments and she didn't have any real education. She worked in a chicken factory, a meat shop.

By the way, when she was in the prison camp, she had a friend who I later found out was a lesbian, although she never spoke openly about it. All her life she [the friend] lived alone, liked to wear pants, smoked unfiltered cigarettes. She always did men's work.

Sonja: Did she have a relationship with your mom?

Sergey: I don't know. I don't think so. She had a very sad life. She tried to get married. She never had any children. She was sent to the camp. Her whole life she worked and worked.

Sonja: When did you first have feelings for boys?

Sergey: Well, I guess it goes back as far as I can remember. I always had these feelings. But I thought that it was wrong, so I tried to repress them. Everyone around me said it was wrong.

Sonja: Then did you say anything about it to your friends?

Sergey: Of course not. But from what they said, I could see perfectly well what they thought about the idea of homosexuality.

Sonja: So when you were in school you already felt you were different from the others?

Sergey: I can't even say what I felt. We lived like one big family. It was only later that I began to understand something wasn't right. I tried to curb myself, I tried to be part of the herd, like everyone else, change myself.

Sonja: This happened when you started to have serious attractions?

Sergey: Yes, there were crushes and sexual relations, but ...well. I didn't think that was right. I even hid these feelings from myself. I consciously tried to get away from it all.

Sonja: Can you talk a little about your first experience?

Sergey: The very first? I don't remember. Honestly, I don't remember. I met my friend Sergey when he was eighteen, I think, and I was twenty or so. We spent eight years together. At first, for about two years, we were just friends, without any sexual contact. And then it happened. But circumstances at that time didn't allow us to live together. We went to visit each other. Nobody suspected anything. Then he moved to Tashkent. I visited him from time to time.

Sonja: Was he married, too?

Sergey: He got married after we separated, but then he got divorced.

Sonja: Do you stay in touch?

Sergey: We write, sometimes call each other. But he lives far away and now it's another country. It's hard to be together.

Sonja: Did you try to live with women, to escape from your homosexuality?

Sergey: I married three times, although not officially, and each time it lasted about a year. After that, I understood that I couldn't.

Sonja: What age was this? Were you twenty or older?

Sergey: Yes, twenty, twenty-five, even over thirty.

Sonja: How did you relate to the women you were married to?

Sergey: I felt a huge weight—a sexual duty. I really felt guilty or that I owed them something. When I realized I'd gone as far as I could, I was on the verge of a nervous breakdown, and I was in bad shape. I would just take off.

Sonja: Did you feel you were on the edge of a nervous breakdown the last time? Or did that happen each time?

Sergey: It ended that way almost every time. I started to drink. I felt bad and I wanted to get away from everyone. I didn't want anyone to touch me. I didn't want to see anyone or know anyone. Then six months would go by, or a year, before I came out of it. It was always hard for me. I must have a very strong nervous system since I could get through that and not go crazy.

Sonja: Did these women guess about the reason for your problems?

Sergey: It's hard to say. They needed sex from me. Just being friends wasn't enough. Now they all know about me. I get along fine with them, we see each other sometimes. I have good relationships with them. They all say that they suspected it, but they hoped to change me.

Sonja: Did you ever go to psychiatrists?

Sergey: About two years ago. I had some kind of psychological problem. It showed up with my speech slowing down, and I felt very lethargic. I went to the doctor and told him everything. They put me in a psychiatric hospital, not really in the hospital itself, but in the attached rehab center. I didn't hide my sexual orientation there and people would point at me. I was some kind of live specimen. At first they gave me pills for lethargy. I began feeling better but then I realized that they were doping me up with some sort of strange medication. I refused to take it and asked to be sent to the hospital for a while. I didn't attempt suicide, it was just difficult. And then I got surprisingly lucky. There was one female psychiatrist who I later found out was a lesbian. She wanted to talk to me, and right away I felt her interest. She talked to me not because it was her job, but to offer help as a human being. I was completely open with her and she helped me a lot. Soon after that, she had to leave. She quit because her colleagues were harassing her. She went to Moscow or Petersburg. Before she left, she came to see me and told me everything about herself. She was someone I really got along well with. If I had ended up with a different psychiatrist, I don't know what would have happened.

Sonja: So how did it all end?

Sergey: They soon let me out. They didn't find any pathology. It was just a nervous breakdown.

Sonja: Did you have any other lesbian friends?

Sergey. Yes, I did. I went to visit one of them when I was feeling bad, near the river Amur. I would swim there, lay out in the sun. I was closeted then and I didn't have anyone to talk to. I talked with her a lot. And there was another one who I could also talk to about my problems.

Sonja: After your last marriage did you decide that you had to find a different way to live?

Sergey: I realized that I couldn't live a double life anymore. In the so-called stagnant years [under Brezhnev], it was the rule. People did one thing at home but at work, in public, they tried to look different. It was very hard for me. I could have gone crazy. One day I had an operation to remove a kidney stone; it was a very difficult operation. I thought: how long do I have to live? And how can I keep living a life not my own? After all, I'm not hurting anyone. If I respect other people's choices, why shouldn't they respect mine? I decided that somehow I'd have to come out. Then I clearly knew what I had to do. I didn't have any career ambitions and I had nothing to lose. Up to now I'd spent all my strength trying to convince the world that I was normal. But maybe my creative potential could be much better used to help myself and others.

So I did that. Some people understood me, some didn't. It was kind of a test, a test for my friends and acquaintances. In the end, some people left my life and real friends stayed, including my brother and other relatives. They all knew about me.

Sonja: How old were you when you came out? Was it hard?

Sergey: Thirty-eight. I was able to come out when I realized that I couldn't depend on anyone. I had my own apartment and I worked for my own bread. I didn't want to lie to people anymore.

Sonja: Where do gay people meet here? You talked about *pleshki* [meeting places].

Sergey: Yes, there are places like that. People often go there, not to pick someone up, but to talk and pour out their souls and see people who understand them. When a person feels bad, when he can't even come out to his family, when his father and mother don't understand him—those are the people who need this kind of interaction.

Sonja: Where does that happen?

Sergey: In our city, people usually meet at the city parks and on Revolution Square. In the summer, people meet there on Saturdays and Sundays. In the winter, it's more in people's apartments. Social groups form, with people who have a similar development, interest, or age. All kinds of people meet there—teachers, doctors, students, the most diverse people.

Sonja: Do you use the terms active and passive [top and bottom]?

Sergey: Yes, we do. And there's also the word "combined" [he used the English word], when someone is both top and bottom, and more of a top.

Sonja: When you meet someone, do you ask him about that or do you just have a feeling about it?

Sergey: I learned to figure it out myself, and I hardly ever make a mistake. It takes one to know one, right? By the way, I try not to start out right away with sex. For me, getting to know a person is the important thing, so that he can understand me and I can understand him.

Sonja: What determines the roles?

Sergey: Probably, it's built into a person. One person likes to be more active and another likes to be more passive. It doesn't depend on age or anything else. The important thing is which role is more your taste. Masochists want to be beaten. Sadists want to beat them. That's how they like it.

Sonja: Have you ever met a trans person? Do you socialize with them?

Sergey: Yes, I do have one friend. She wants to have a sex change, she's saving up for it. The operation is very expensive. Since childhood she's felt like a man. She has a masculine walk, haircut, speech. Even the poetry she writes is masculine. She does body building. She can't refer to herself as she. She hides from the people around her. She wants to earn enough money for the operation, but now it's difficult. In general, sex changes are very hard.

Sonja: Tell me what led you to decide to start the Astarte organization.

Sergey: I never went to the so-called *pleshki*, where gay people get together; I wanted a different level of interaction. One day my friend Natasha, a lesbian, introduced me to some guys who wanted to have a more or less serious organization. I volunteered to help them because I had some experience with organizing. I told them, "When a person is alone, you can fire him, evict him, even kill him. You can do whatever you want to him. He can disappear without a trace. But when you have an organization, this is harder to do. We need to have official status as an organization. We need to learn how to defend our rights. We should be able to be in any area of life—in everyday life, at work, in politics—and openly give our opinions on any social problem. I'm sick of gathering in basements, meeting people in bathrooms. I know how this is done." We started to work. We wrote a charter and gathered the necessary number of signatures for official registration. We registered the organization in the Department of Justice.

How were we able to do it? In Russia, the state carries out various campaigns. There may be an anti-alcohol campaign and we all give up drinking. Grapevines are cut down and wine cellars get sealed up. We don't drink! Then democracy comes along. New campaigns, everyone can do anything! When we came, they said to us, "You can do it! Come on! You'll have your organization!" We got into all this and I'm glad we did, otherwise nothing would have come of it. But then the campaigns ended and everything became much harder. We still can't open a bank account and we've been running around for three years. Officials just made us run around in circles. I can show you a whole packet of documents that I've kept over the years, all the signatures. They've brought up various laws, bylaws, they plead ignorance, something is missing. Then suddenly they say we still need to go here or there. You didn't register in the right place; you don't live there anymore. Naturally, we don't have enough money for all this. What can you do with meager membership dues? Print a few informational brochures and that's it. We tried going through the government, but they have different aims and tasks. According to them, the most important work of our anti-AIDS organization would be to make a list of people with a certain sexual orientation.

So it's very hard for me. They don't let us do our work. We had a couple of dances. We wrote official letters asking for permission to meet, we paid rent, but it worked out only because I personally was able to convince the administrator. He values me because he thinks I'm useful. After the dance, he got so much pressure from higher ups, that he told me frankly, "Listen, I don't know how what to do with you now." I'm afraid I'll have to leave this job, too. They've already barred me from the Cultural Regional Committee. They could force me out of here too. Maybe they want to get rid of me completely? I don't know. I work with gay people and lesbians who live in this city. But to those who live in the outer regions, I tell them outright that it's too early to come out. Only to your parents, to get rid of psychological barriers, but to everyone else, no. I don't know how much time will pass before it will be possible.

Sonja: How many dances did you have?

Sergey: Quite a few. Usually we have one dance every two months. We also had some very interesting celebrations. At our first dance, riot police burst in with all their weapons, waved around machine guns, intimidating people: "We're rounding up all of you!" The precinct captain has come several times. I talked to him for a bit and showed him our permit. He said, "For now you guys can dance. Go ahead, dance, later we'll see..." I was even able to organize a dance in the Sports Palace, a big hall for seven thousand people, I called it: Dance While You're Young! I was completely responsible for everything that went on.

Sonja: How many people usually come?

Sergey: Fifty to a hundred.

Sonja: More gay men than lesbians?

Sergey: Yes, more gay men. Women are afraid to come out. It's probably harder for them to make the move.

Sonja: Were things worse before? Have you heard anything about that?

Sergey: There were criminal prosecutions. Once in Tomsk they arrested a whole group of artists and intellectuals. It was a very big operation. There were employees of the television studio, people who had high positions, some even killed themselves. Of course, that affected me very much. I began to hide as much as I could. Nobody knew anything about me. I had minimal sexual contact.

Sonja: When was this?

Sergey: In the seventies.

Sonja: Was there anything like it in other cities?

Sergey: I don't know. I don't have information about other regions. And even here the operation was closed to the public and it wasn't written about in the papers. But they couldn't completely silence it. Too many well-known people ended up in prison or gave up on life.

Sonja: Do you know anyone who went to prison then?

Sergey: I know a few people whose lives were destroyed. They were convicted and after they were released they lost their right to live in the city. They had to live in the country in a small area, where people knew everything about each other. People treated them very badly and their spirits were destroyed, not to mention prison. There, gays are not considered people. They're beasts, who are given the most humiliating work. They are used by everyone. It's the whole system that oppresses us: since you're gay, we're going to order you around the way we want. It's a typical means of oppression in a totalitarian regime, and not only in totalitarian ones.

Sonja: Do you think anything has changed since then?

Sergey: Almost nothing. The forms of oppression have become more refined. They don't put you in jail now, but they don't let you work normally either. You won't be promoted and they can fire you at any moment. They can really bring you down. I am constantly painting over graffiti on doors. They whisper behind your back. It's hard, really hard. One day I talked about these problems to an administrator from the regional headquarters. I asked him right out what he thought about gays. He answered, "I would convict all of you or hang you."

Sonja: Haven't there been some changes since *perestroika*?

Sergey: Of course, there's more freedom to express your feelings and thoughts. You don't have to whisper in the kitchen anymore. They don't convict you for talking now. Life itself has changed. Before, it was clearly written what you could do and couldn't do. If I had done this kind of interview in the eighties, the next day I'd be fired, imprisoned or exiled. Now I can give interviews and tell people about my sexual orientation. But really, in our society not much has changed. The same people are in power now as under Communism. And it's still not clear whether this will last for a while or whether it will all be over tomorrow. Someone could come along and say: "Alright, you guys, enough of this freedom. Onward to communism, single file!" And we all go. Can it happen? It can—it's completely possible. The political situation in the country is very unpredictable. And it's become more corrupt. Now everything's up for sale. For something to seriously change, a new generation needs to come to power that knows the taste of freedom and knows its cost. We were raised in the old traditions. We speak while looking over our shoulders checking on someone else's opinion, afraid that people will get the wrong impression. We lived in barracks for seventy years, we got used to walking in formation. We've produced things. I don't know what. Redirected rivers to I don't know where, and now we don't know what to do. Our city is a radioactive bomb with a slow fuse. All that needs to change.

The attitude toward gays is all mixed up in that. A person who's not like others is a threat to the established order. Naturally, they try to push him away or get rid of him completely. That's more the issue, not just traditional ethical norms. Why won't they let me speak and inform people about what I think is necessary, at least from a medical point of view? Again, the root of all this is political: "We need to be careful nothing happens. We can't allow that." They're afraid of everyone who cannot be programmed or bought. It's the Russian government's usual fear. Keep everyone in check. Give someone an apartment, or scare a person. They are in power, and there they eat well. They make deals to the depths of the earth, they even deal in people's intellects—left and right. They have Swiss bank accounts, their children are all set. So why should they change anything?

The issue is not at all with my sexual orientation. It's a deeper question. I don't want to join the herd. I'm not a sheep. I want to live a normal life. I want to work where I like and get paid what I'm worth. I want to travel abroad. I don't know how to steal, so there's only one thing left—work.

Sonja: You told me that Siberia is not Moscow and not St. Petersburg. So what do you think is the difference?

Sergey: Russian politics takes place in Moscow but Muscovites don't understand that in Siberia people are totally different. They, the center, are cut off from the people. In Moscow and Petersburg they don't understand our needs; they don't understand what we want. They think up laws for themselves and believe they're good for everyone. But we have a different way of thinking, different customs and traditions. Here people are more sedate, it takes a long time to get them to do something. To tell you the truth, Tomsk is the sanctuary of the era of stagnation. Yegor Ligachev was in charge here for many years, the most conservative public figure of the *perestroika* years. Russia got to the point of simply breaking apart. Not long ago, they wrote the Siberian agreement, which opposed the central power structure, and many Siberian cities joined. If a critical mass, dissatisfied with Moscow, comes together, it would be scary. Anything could happen.

Sonja: What historical events impacted your life?

Sergey: Sex life? Or life in general?

Sonja: Both.

Sergey: Of course, *perestroika*. I'm grateful to Gorbachev for what he did. If he hadn't started the reforms, who knows where we would have gone. I think in any case I would have tried to change my life. I don't know that I would have been able to do what I've done now. The constitutional crisis in October of 1993 also greatly affected me. You can't get away from politics. All of Russia is affected. Politics dictates the conditions of our lives. I can't separate myself from others.

Sonja: More than a few Russian artists, singers, historical figures are gay. Do you like any of them?

Sergey: I don't know where to start. If you mean famous ones, it's Tchaikovsky. I feel very close to his music. Contemporary figures—I like Penkin and Moiseev. Then people talk about Laima Vaikule. Although she isn't Russian, we think of her as one of our [meaning queer] singers. We all love her. I could also mention Elton John and many others. I know the gay intelligentsia of Tomsk very well. People in entertainment, in the arts, science. There are many, a few hundred. I've spent time with almost all of them. They're very intelligent people and they can do a lot.

Sonja: Do you want to add anything?

Sergey: About what I've said? I don't know. I'd like to address the people who will read this interview, to say that we're grateful for the attention that you have given us, for the opportunity to talk about our lives. We will live on. We want society not to suppress us, like it does now—the society we live in. We would like to change that. We would like to do something for everyone. But I'm glad that I live here and at this time. I want to be happy, and God willing that will happen.

Victor

Interviewed in 1995
Translated by Sonja Franeta

A tall, handsome man with blonde hair, Victor lives with his boyfriend in their newly renovated, comfortable apartment in the center of Novosibirsk. We spoke in his kitchen. He is a waiter by profession and for a time he worked in railroad restaurant cars, traveling throughout the Soviet Union. Born in Almaty in 1950, he is Ukrainian by nationality, but he lives, like most of his family, in Novosibirsk.

Sonja: Tell me a little bit about yourself and your parents.

Victor: My mother was a house painter. My father was also a painter. In those days, as general workers, painters made good money. On the whole, they didn't live too badly. When I was seven, we moved to Almaty. A lot of land was available there. The Germans from the Volga Area, the Ingush people, and the Chechens settled there. That's where we lived. I finished eighth grade in 1968. Then my mother and father divorced, my mother returned here [Novosibirsk] to her mother, my grandmother. I finished school in Novosibirsk and then technical school for culinary arts and hospitality. Then I went to work in my specialty as a waiter. At that time, this was profitable work. The standard monthly salary was eighty rubles and sometimes you could earn this in one day. Waiters, administrators, warehouse people, salesman did a lot better at the time than ordinary engineers or factory workers. Everything you see here is a result of my waiter's salary.

Sonja: Did your family come to Siberia originally from the Ukraine?

Victor: Yes, my grandmother did. Actually my grandmother's relatives arrived here before the revolution during the time of the Stolypin land reforms. According to this reform Siberia was supposed to get settled, so they came here to Siberia for free land. After the Tsar's declaration, they were given money to settle this land. That's how my family came here. My grandfather was a local Siberian. The people who came were called *Katsapy* but my grandfather was an original resident.

Sonja: Were you a Pioneer and a Komsomol member?

Victor: Yes, I wore a red tie. Then I became a Komsomol member. We were required to join the Komsomol. Nothing actually had to be done—we just had to pay membership fees. Almost all the youth had to go into the Komsomol. But I was in for only about three years and then left. I never became a member of the Party. Nevertheless, they would not let me join the Party because I was sixteen but already under the watch of the KGB, as a gay man.

Sonja: How did that happen? How did they find out about you?

Victor: Actually, I came out as gay at the age of sixteen. I got to know a man who was twenty-two years old. For me all of this was new. He was an actor and he introduced me to his social group. Now, they had had problems with the KGB. They were all arrested but then couldn't't get convicted. When I came along I was the youngest in the group but I was underage. Everything rested on my testimony. They called me in and they scared me pretty badly. I explained everything that happened, about the sex and so forth. They said: you're young, you're only sixteen, you won't be imprisoned for this, and neither will they, nothing will happen to them. I believed them because I was stupid and young. After that they ordered all of them to prison. But thank God, among my friends, there were some good ones who were still free. They came to my house. They told my mother everything. They explained to her how I should have conducted myself at the questioning. They asked my mother to persuade me to change my testimony for the trial. I came home and saw that my mother was sitting with my friend and his comrades. My mother had a very strange look on her face, like she was crying. She told me that she knew everything and we had to rescue my friends.

They told me how to retract my previous testimony. When it was my turn to talk, I said what they told me to say, but everything was not ok. It all turned out different—what happened. The guy started knocking on the table, scaring me, saying that things will be bad for me in there, and all the rest. But they [my friends] had warned me: let him say what he wants but you have to change your testimony. I did so no matter how they scared me. I stayed on course. They imprisoned me for two days in a holding cell, just to scare me, and because I was young and it was my first encounter with the police. I survived all of it. In court I said everything I had to to get them all released. And they actually released all of them, after threatening them with six or seven years.

I have a friend living here in Novosibirsk. He celebrated his fifty-fifth birthday not too long ago. He spent seventeen years in prison for that very law [Article 121]. I am so envious that with his age and after spending so much time in prison, he still has so much spirit and optimism. He would be the envy of anyone his age, without even setting foot in prison.

Sonja: Do you keep in touch with your first boyfriend? Is he still gay?

Victor: Yes, he is still gay. He's a doctor, a leading doctor in Novosibirsk. He lives with his mother. Of course, for a while after that incident we didn't speak. He was very hurt that I told everything. When we started speaking again, I explained all of it—that I was only sixteen, that I couldn't have known what was going on, and what they were asking me. Now we are friends. We call each other and visit.

Sonja: How did your mother and brother react to your being gay? You have a brother?

Victor: Yes, one. He's eight years younger than me. As I said before, my mother found out about everything very early. That's how my brother found out. Everything happened on its own; I didn't need to explain things. My friends came over to visit and my mother went over to their homes, too. She figured out quickly that gays were not the hooligans everyone said they were, that they are normal and good people. And my brother also began to socialize with them. He'd say hi all the time and wasn't shy about it; he even defends them. When people talk about someone I know and say, "Oh, he's gay." My brother would say, "So what's wrong with that? What business do we have looking into someone else's bed?" That's how it should be.

Sonja : What does your brother do for a living?

Victor: He is a businessman. Before, he was a bartender, following in my footsteps.

Sonja: And what about your father?

Victor: When my parents divorced, he stayed in Almaty. I never saw my father again. I don't really know him; he never came here.

Sonja: When did you feel attracted to men?

Victor: I can't really say the exact age. Since I was about five, six, or maybe ten years old. I was born that way. I remember in the eighth grade I was intuitively in love with a classmate, but he had no interest. We had some kind of exploratory sex. I didn't know that I was gay then. I didn't even know the concept. But I never regretted it. I never judged myself like some of my friends or wondered why I was that way. Other people live a normal life—a family, car, a dacha, children. I have lived this way for forty-five years and never regretted it. It's because I've met good people and I've socialized with gays. They're more open, more honest. They would help me in a difficult time. It's more interesting with them. Even in hard times you could go to any town and find help anywhere. Let's say you're going to Samarkand, or Tashkent, or even Moscow or Leningrad. You can get contacts. They'll even meet you, put you up, feed you, and show you things of interest. In the gay community we try to support one another. If I wasn't gay, I would hardly even know some things or see what I've seen. Everything is because of help from my brothers, even materially.

Sonja: How did you connect with other gays before? How did you know one another?

Victor: The important thing was it was *our community*. Through my friends I got to know other people, my future friends. There are certain places where gays could go to get to know one another, often in the park. At the very center [of Novosibirsk], *Pervomayski Park* [First of May Park]. Awesome. We'd spend evenings there; we'd talk and walk around, go together to the café. You know, before, it was much safer and more interesting. Many people who remember the past can confirm this.

Now it's very difficult to live. There are robbers, thieves, bandits. At that time people were ill-informed and they didn't really get into those things. It wasn't a concern to regular people if you're blue [gay], green, or red, as long as the person is good. Even now, hardly anyone knows anything about it. There's very little information, no written material. Yet everyone is trying to put their noses in our business. Even the police related to us better before: "Just as long as he doesn't go beyond the law." Well, they also tried, of course, to scare us. They'd take someone in for questioning, someone they didn't like. Just like at the time of that operation, when I was sixteen years old.

I remember one incident in Akademgorodok, near Novosibirsk, working in a hotel restaurant there. At the time many listen to Voice of America programs and to the BBC in Russian, even though it was forbidden. One day I came to work and stupidly bragged about listening to Voice of America. They reported me. One of the waiters was a snitch. The next day I was called into the KGB. They said: if you are going to talk about what you listen to at night, how about seeing what it's like to be gay in prison? That served as a very good reminder not to talk at work about anything I had heard. Not with other gays, of course, but at work. I could say anything openly among our own.

Of course, they couldn't put me in prison just for listening to Voice of America. But for being gay they could. How those people suffered during that investigation! They would've been put in prison, if I had not changed my testimony. These were well-known people. In town they were important and many people talked about them. They were the intelligentsia and knew a lot and read a lot and listened and talked.

Naturally they wanted to get rid of some of them. But how could they? Imprison them for listening to Voice of America or for reading literature? That's not against the law; they could only be imprisoned for being gay.

Sonja: Did you have friends who ended up in prison?

Victor: Yes, the one I told you about. He's fifty-five years old and he was in prison three times, altogether seventeen years.

Sonja: And were there other situations like that in Novosibirsk?

Victor: It was not unusual. I had another friend who was imprisoned. After prison he couldn't get a job anywhere. It never even showed up in his documents what law he was imprisoned for. In the past, he worked in a research institute. He couldn't get another job like that. He only had that one profession. He couldn't work as a laborer, because he had higher education. In the end, all his relatives found out, his wife, his colleagues from a previous job. He ended up killing himself. Another good friend who was in prison was crippled, not physically but psychologically. He became a drunk. Another one, a physics and math teacher went to prison twice under this law, for seven or eight years. He was a famous teacher, but he was fired and not allowed to work in a school, even though he never had any relationships with minors. He had to join the business world. He died not too long ago.

Sonja: Tell me a little about your school life. Were there other boys or girls there who felt that they were not like the others?

Victor: Yes, I had a friend like that in school, but we had no idea what we were. We were drawn to each other subconsciously. He never hung out with girls. We were always together. After me he only hung out with the boys. I myself was sixteen when I figured out I was gay.

Sonja: Were you friends because of this?

Victor: We had similar interests, similar ideas. I told you, we were drawn to each other subconsciously.

Sonja: How did you decide to get married [to a woman]?

Victor: I became acquainted with my bride in a very strange way. It was at a dance. I had been going there with my friends, my gay friends. We'd dance and then hang out in our different groups. I brought her over to my group. When a woman shows up in a group of gays, it's like a new spirit, new energy. Do you know what I mean? They treated her better and she sensed it right away. She liked being put on a pedestal, figuratively speaking. When we were eighteen we got married. I told her right away, "Lyuba, you know that I'm gay. Do you realize what kind of a life you're going to have?" She said: "Those are your issues, let it be your hobby, like playing cards, or dominoes or chess. Most important is that you don't see another woman. If I find out that you're with another woman, there'll be a scandal." That's exactly how she related to me. She always accepted my friends in our apartment. We went on vacations together and stayed at people's homes together. When we went to other cities we always stayed with gay friends. Since then, she has only socialized with gays, and not only because she got used to it. She feels that these people are the kind of people she can be with. Sexually she's frigid, she doesn't actually need sex. For her, what's most important is socializing. She knows very well that in a gay social group she would be well taken care of and no one would attempt to get her into bed.

I have a daughter, almost twenty years old, a good young woman. She knows everything about me. I told my wife right away that I didn't want to hide these things from her, because, all the same, things would come out into the open. It's better that she find this out from her parents not from some neighbor or from some lowlife gossip. That's what we did. As she grew up, she understood everything very well. Of course her mother also spoke about these subjects with her. It was like something was passed down to her. All of her friends are gay. She says she goes everywhere with them and is not be afraid in any of those circles. She's never mistreated. Not long ago, I asked her if she was getting married. She said no, I can wait a little, no need to rush. I'll probably take the same step as mom. I'll marry a gay man. She said that just the other day.

Sonja: Is it possible that your wife is a lesbian?

Victor: No. After me, after we got divorced, she got close to a young man who was also gay.

Sonja: Is she married now?

Victor: No, no, she lives with her mother and our daughter. The three of them run a private club.

Sonja: How was your relationship with your wife?

Victor: When we got married, there were some conditions. I said: Lyuba, you know I like young people, so you can see it won't be easy. She said she understood; she agreed because she loved me. Honestly, I never felt love for her. I just got used to her. She has a very easygoing personality. I served in the army in Khabarovsk, quite far from Novosibirsk. She left her job and went there in order to work near me. She bribed my supervisor to let me have a break a few days at a time. Anyway, I only served five or six months in the army.

Sonja: Did you get released from military duty?

Victor: Yes, they transferred me to the reserve because of the gay law. My friend from Kiev sent me a letter and showed me how to do it. I had to send a letter to the military hospital, pretending to be attracted to our cook. I wrote such a letter and sent it not through the army mail but in the regular mail, so that my immediate supervisors would not find out. About two weeks later, a car arrived and they took me to a hospital. My commanding officer asked right in front of me: what is the reason you taking him? They said: an examination. They took me to the hospital and then right away sent me to the reserve. I repeated what I said in the letter. They kept me in the hospital a couple of days in order to fill out paperwork. They transferred me out because of Law 7B—psychopathology. Actually, this law has no connection to homosexuality whatsoever. When I came back the officer asked why they transferred me. They had told me in the hospital not to tell anyone anything. I said: I don't know, some documents came from Novosibirsk and here they are. After the hospital, they transferred me. Everyone was surprised they let me leave the army so easily.

Sonja: So nowhere in the documents did it say you were homosexual?

Victor: No. the only thing there was the name of the Law 7B.

Sonja: Did this give you any problems later?

Victor: I didn't think it would hurt me. I already knew I was on the KGB lists as a homosexual from the age of sixteen. My work was never connected with any kind of secrets. I worked as a waiter, then a restaurant manager. They knew about me at work. I never really hid it from anyone. There was no reason to hide: the police knew and the KGB knew. My mother knew from the very beginning, my brother too. The only thing I was worried about was some kind of entrapment on the part of the KGB. But I tried not to cross any sexual boundaries with men. I only went with close friends from my own circle. I never picked up anyone on the street. If I felt that someone was behaving a little strangely, I'd cut off relations. So [in a Russian sign for good luck, he spits three times], thank God, I never went to prison for that.

Sonja: If homosexual relations were forbidden by law, if everyone was so afraid of Article 121, how did you feel so confident?

Victor: What can I say? Article 121 was meant to be only for sodomy, That is, only for anal sex. If, for example, I only did oral sex, they couldn't put me in prison. That actually saved me. No, I always said I had nothing to do with sodomy. Also, there were all kinds of nuances regarding the law, so one could get out of going to prison. Let's say, at the hearing someone says there was anal sex; there has to be a second witness. On the other hand, if there were no witnesses, it would be hard to get convicted. Of course, some ended up in prison for stupid reasons—they'd say, okay, I'm going to report this and say we slept together—he's a bad person, and so forth. Then he could be convicted. After that you still had to have two witnesses in order to confirm it. The

KGB, of course, used various methods. Sometimes they paid witnesses. If they really wanted to put someone in prison they could do that anytime they wanted. For example, if he annoyed someone higher up. If you were cozy with the law and kept your mouth shut, if you didn't say that you were listening to or reading something forbidden, you could stay out of prison.

Sonja: You figured out you were gay when you were young. How could you accept this revelation about yourself so easily?

Victor: The fact of the matter is, it was not a big revelation. I don't know, I was ready, since the age of five to ten, within myself. I knew that sooner or later it would happen. Therefore, when I slept with a man for the first time and told him that he was my first one, he didn't believe me. He said, why are you lying to me? I see you're a professional. I'll say it again, I was ready both psychologically and spiritually. I was expecting it, even intuitively.

Sonja: How long did you live with your wife?

Victor: Fifteen years.

Sonja: Did you live like family?

Victor: Yes, just like a normal Soviet couple. In the same apartment, with the same cares, the same money, and one child. We had a small space, a one room apartment [with a kitchen]. The four of us lived together: my mother-in-law, us and our child. I continued to have sex with men, of course, but not in front of my family. Sometimes I didn't spend the night at home, but I let them know I was staying somewhere else. My wife totally understood what that meant. We had visitors, too, at home, naturally, but nothing special.

Sonja: What were you doing at the time?

Victor: A restaurant manager.

Sonja: You never had any problems at work?

Victor: There were some problems, but not very serious. Someone could be mean and say such and such about me. I never paid any attention to that, which irritated the guy even more. He could tell that he didn't get to me with that; he said it once, twice, and then got tired of it. Everything would go back to normal. I don't want to pump myself up, but I was always in good standing at work. They never paid attention to the things people said. But I could tell they were saying things behind my back. There's a cafe in our city called Sputnik. I worked as a manager there. Everybody knew that gays came around, even our management knew. But it wasn't easy to get a seat. You had to reserve a table in advance in order to have dinner or eat supper. Everybody knew we had good quality meals and good service. All the service people were gay or gay-friendly. That's why the atmosphere at work was so free and easy. Any of our Novosibirsk friends would know this cafe. For example, our friend in common, Andrey, loved going there. Yes, and all the young gays would go to that cafe. You could relax with no problem, meet your friends, and socialize. Practically the whole town knew this was a gay cafe. And there were never any roundups or repression there.

Sonja: Were there other places where gays met?

Victor: There weren't any special places. First of May Park was in the center of town, where you could meet people, socialize, and have fun.

Sonja: Did new people go there?

Victor: Yes, for example, if someone came to Novosibirsk from Moscow or Leningrad, they would be told: if you want to find gays go to the First of May Park. These days they meet one another near the theater. Everyone knows you can find gays and lesbians there.

Sonja: Do you know the term coming out?

Victor: No.

Sonja: It means to be open about yourself. What do you think about that? Did you ever want to tell friends and acquaintances, including heterosexuals, that you were gay?

Victor: I have a lot of [straight] friends who know. I have friends who can't imagine how I could sleep with a man. But they are completely cool about it, they don't care what I do at night. For them what's important is that I am a friend and comrade. They know everything about me; they know I have gay friends and they still socialize with me. They're not afraid that I am not like them.

Sonja: In the past, did people talk about this openly?

Victor: No, of course not. They didn't speak about it or write about it at all. People didn't know anything about it. Gays just kept to themselves. There were no publications, all the news went around completely like rumors. For example, we had no idea that there were clubs for gays in America or in England, and all the rest,. What in God's name would it mean to have clubs or weddings or that a man could have a civil union with another man? That was unimaginable for us. Many of our people feared that people would find out at work. Many men even got married to women unwillingly. Some did this in order to get into the Party and have a career. In order to go abroad at that time you had to have a wife and children. Many led a double life. You have no need for a woman and yet you were living with one. And her life is ruined as well as yours. God help you if she finds out something—then it's a complete tragedy. Many people destroyed their lives that way, became alcoholics, even took their own lives. If someone had a more or less big responsibility, with a good job, it was very difficult to hide his real feelings. That's why there were circles, where only six or seven people could socialize. They were there among themselves in a private apartment. And to get into those groups and sit at the same table with them, you needed to go through some steps, gain their trust. I knew some of them. One worked with us here in town in the Komsomol, another one in the Party executive committee. In the past, they were afraid of any kind of rumors, to the point that they never came to those places to meet other gays.

Back then, when I would go to Vilnius [Lithuania], I had to get a residency card to get a job and a place to live. My friend who drove me there got me the residency through his friend who worked in the KGB.

Gays were in the KGB then. He even helped me with getting work. Not knowing the Lithuanian language, it was very difficult to become a cafe or restaurant manager. But they accepted me at an OK restaurant, where it was hard even for a Lithuanian to get a job. There were also a few gays in the police department. Others got into the justice system and all were connected.

Sonja: Do you have lesbian friends?

Victor: Until *perestroika*, I did not know even one lesbian. I guess they had their own social groups, just like the gays had theirs. There was always talk, of course. For example, some women would walk together and my friends would say: look, Victor, there's a lesbian. But we didn't socialize with them. We would not sit at the same table like this, never. Even now I don't know very many, but there is more mixing. Before, there was none of that. They socialized by themselves and we were separate.

Sonja: You said there weren't any particular problems at work. Why did you leave your last job?

Victor: That was a different job. I can't work in my specialty anymore. Times are different. In the past, a waiter or restaurant manager were important people, now they are only service people. Who goes to restaurants now? Only people with illegal money, mafia types, skinheads. I had to look for another line of work, so I got a job as a salesman in a store. I have a good salary, and I can even buy and sell things independently. One time, I brought home some things from Turkey. The store owner invited herself over to see what I had. We sat around and had tea but she didn't say anything in particular. Then I heard rumors going around: Victor Ivanovich is about to get a Mercedes but I can't even afford a mixer for my kitchen. She started getting jealous. I got paid less and less. They forbid me to sell things on the side. I decided to talk with her openly. I asked: what is the meaning of all this? She said: you live very well and I don't have anything. I said to her: I'm living in a cooperative apartment—the furniture, the rugs were all bough earlier. I am forty-five years old and you're only twenty-eight—isn't that a big difference? You're a businessperson who climbed up on the *perestroika* ladder. If it weren't for *perestroika*, you would never have become a store owner. I worked hard for everything, while you were still a toddler under a table. It's just pure jealousy, piles of Russian envy. In short, I got mad at her and quit.

Sonja: Do you think she changed her attitude because you were gay?

Victor: No, she knew from the very first day I was hired that I lived with Dima [my boyfriend]. We come and go together, we shop together. It was obvious we were a gay couple. If she didn't want to hire us both, she didn't have to. I got involved in all this through friends and they probably said something to her about my being gay. Do you or don't you want us to work? She took us. We worked for one year and everything was OK.

I know this too, because not long ago she asked me and Dima to come back to the store with her. I still hadn't posed the question about salaries then. She had some problems with her partner or co-worker and they parted ways. They were stealing from each other. Actually, her partner oversold things and fooled around with the numbers. That's businesspeople for you!

Sonja: Did you have those kinds of problems where you were working before?

Victor: No, not really. In general, life has worked out for me. There was no repression, either from the KGB or the police. And with friends it has all worked out—none of them, by and large, have betrayed me. At work too, there haven't been any intrigues. Although I've heard about many cases of other gay men. I know a lot of horrible things have happened. I'm a very social person, very communicative. I find a way to talk to everyone. In my youth I was threatened at times: hey, you, queer, we'll beat you up and so on. But whether it was my way with words or whatever, something always saved me. I socialized with all kinds of people when I worked in the restaurant. A lot of them knew I was gay. Even the simplest people always talked with me, even those who wanted nothing to do with gays.

Sonja: So there were times when you were threatened?

Victor: Not really threatened, but afraid of being under the scrutiny of the KGB. For a time I worked in a restaurant in Sochi, where foreigners came to eat. There I got to know an American. But going to his room was nearly impossible for we were not allowed to go to foreigners' rooms. I could only speak to him a little bit at dinnertime, very quietly, because there were recorders everywhere. We managed to arrange a secret meeting. We met at some far corner of the beach. Rarely but occasionally, there was a way to go into hotel rooms. The people who guarded the floors and the receptionists also had to take breaks for dinner. We are all human beings. It was possible to make arrangements not to inform the chain of command that I went into someone's room. But I never got together with my American friend in his room. We spent the night at my place. When his group took a trip somewhere out of town, he told his guide that his head hurt and he was going to the beach. But really he came over to my place or we went far away to some beach, where neither friends nor the KGB could find us. If I had felt that I was being followed, I would have stopped the encounters. I could have had terrible problems. Again God had mercy on me.

Then I had a very intense correspondence with him. I went home to Novosibirsk and he to America. I received letters from him almost daily. He often took business trips and mailed me postcards. Then suddenly the correspondence stopped. I figured out that our letters were pulled from the mail. I wasn't supposed to correspond with him. About two years passed. Then I wrote a letter and the correspondence resumed. But every time he wrote me two letters, I only got one. I would send three and he got one. Later, when I worked in Akademgorodok in the Intourist Hotel, I found a foreigner who could take my letters out of the country and mail them. A lot of foreigners came through to go to seminars and conferences. I knew the letters would get to him that way.

Sonja: How do you relate to the words active and passive? Do you use them?

Victor: No, never. What's active? What's passive? They are just prison jargon. It's what the police use. When they had the big roundup under Article 121, they divided up people according to these categories. If you are active, we'll give you two more years, if passive, two years less. But in life, how could I be only active and my partner only passive. That's only for heterosexuals. If two gay men get together, everything has to be mutual, then it's great. You can't be just active or just passive. That's what I think. One time when I was in a group of guys, someone said I was exclusively active. I went for his throat right away. That simply cannot be. If you are gay, you can't know ahead of time what kind of sex you'll have with another person, whether active or passive. I've always felt that way.

Sonja: Did you ever encounter any sadomasochists?

Victor: No, but do you see the whip hanging there? About ten years ago the Moscow Circus came through. I got to know an artist, a horseback rider. I think he was into that. When I was in bed with him, he tried to do something in such a role, but right away I said no. I never came across anything like that again.

Sonja: Do you have any acquaintances who are into that? Maybe you don't know.

Victor: I don't know. There's a newspaper here, with gay personal ads. It is clearly stated what each person prefers. I have never met up with any of these people. I don't like that.

Sonja: Do you get any information from the West about the gay movement?

Victor: I tried to connect with ILGA [European gay and lesbian organization]. I got an address for them and in the end they sent me last year's catalog. It would be good to make an affiliate here or a small organization. I would be happy to do this. I have the resources. I am not afraid. The time has passed when I was afraid. But I don't have the right materials and literature, and I don't know how exactly to do it. If there was a serious initiative, I would do something. Right now, I only have some close friends. I haven't really increased my circle of friends because today everywhere there are criminals. A long time ago if someone were to take someone's hat or beat him up, it was a sensation in town. In the past, if a gay person stole something from another gay man, it would mean nothing. Nowadays, if a gay man steals from another gay man, it's equivalent to murder. I myself was robbed, actually it was a break-in to my apartment, a tip from some gays. Who else would know that I lived alone? What could I have worth stealing?

Sonja: If you had an organization, what would you want to do?

Victor: First of all, I am well-known among gay men in town as a decent person. Secondly, young people are drawn to me. Like, for example, Andrey, our mutual acquaintance. A lot of young people come to me for advice. I am open with everyone and I have a lot of experience. If there were someone who wanted to help organize all this, if it were clear what to do and how to start, but the way it is now, we have nothing to start with. People are drawn to me, but I can only use my own experience. In the West there are solid organizations that help gays. We are helpless. Now that the gay law is repealed, the police are still the police, uncultured, backward. We don't want material help but we do need literature, interaction, and information.

What do I dream of? Let's say, a group of gay visitors came to us—we could bring them around to Siberia or the Altai region. There are so many beautiful places here. We could organize this and put together a cultural program. Or perhaps some gay man would come here to visit, we would show him where to go. We could have a certain itinerary and he would know where he was safe and where he would not be robbed or hurt. We would be able to get some information from him, too. Now, if I were to go to some foreign country, I wouldn't know where to go or who to turn to, although I could go to the train station and carry a sign saying: I'm gay, help me, be a friend. It would also be good to have a correspondence with someone. We could include something like this in our program.

Sonja: What did gays and lesbians call themselves before and how do they refer to themselves now?

Victor: Before? We never knew the word "gay." The word "blue" [gay] also did not make an appearance until recently. Before, they didn't call us anything. In Russian, we only had pejorative terms: *petukh* [rooster] and *pedik* [fag or pederast].

Sonja: Weren't there some actors in the old days who were gay?

Victor: Jean Marais was thought to be gay, yet no one knew for sure. There were rumors that he was the leader of an entire organization that was gay. But that was in my youth, the old days. Then there's the Muslim singer Magomayev, [from Azerbaijan, the Soviet Sinatra] a well-known, topnotch, opera singer trained in Italy, who was big on the Soviet stage. I really don't know if he was gay or not. Who else? Biser Kirov, also a singer, from Bulgaria.

Sonja: How did the political reforms in Russia affect you?

Victor: Everything was quiet before, even peaceful. Maybe, more accurately, static. You always knew, if you worked you would receive your money. If you got sick, you would be paid, even on sick leave. Now there is constant stress. It shakes up every family, every individual. If you don't have money, it shakes you up. What goes on in Moscow means nothing to people. Just give me food and work. Everything depends on you. In some ways it might be better than the old days. But I consider myself a man of the static years. I always tell other gay men: it was better for gays in the old days. We were much more friendly and open. There wasn't a big iron door then, but an ordinary door with a little lock. And now when you go up to answer the door, you have to ask three times—who is it, what do you want? No one can come to my place now without calling, for example. They call from town—I'll be there at twelve. I look through the peephole to see who it is and then open the door. If you open the door and it's someone you don't know, you might get a punch in the nose or get robbed.

In the past, there were a lot of bad things but also good things. I was never afraid to be out of work. For better or worse, work was always there. On the other hand, I did worry when I was out of work for a long time. Then you'd be called a parasite. Whose money do you live on? These days no one cares whether you work or not, whether you eat or not. I look at the past with some regret. Now they say: freedom of the press! But what do we have for a press? The only thing we have for gays in Novosibirsk is a little newspaper where we can post personals. I want to meet someone. That's all the freedom we have. If you see a Russian gay magazine around, it's usually a copy of something from the West, a reprint sometimes. That's it. Crude content, filthy photos. The kind of quality you don't even want to hold in your hands. But serious material which you would want to read and learn from, we don't have. To this day we get fed gossip and wild guesses. That's why I wanted to have some kind of organization, so we could at least have some legitimate information.

Of course, it's good that we don't have that law any more. Sex is OK within the confines of the law, not with minors, of course. What's the point? The same problems we had are still here. There is nowhere to get together. Let's have a little cafe in the center of town at least, where gays and lesbians can go. There we can have our own mafia paid by gays. A couple of times after you are seen at the cafe, you get pegged as a gay person and you have to pay them or else you get slammed against a wall somewhere and get a talking to. Earlier, in the Sputnik Cafe people got together freely. The whole town knew that only gay people went there. There was no repression, no pay offs. And the police? Well, I remember I was called into the police, when a gay guy was killed. I was already registered with them. They called everyone who was on file with the police or the KGB. What if someone had some information to solve the murder? Yes, the police somehow did its job. But now all they do is beat them up, extort, steal their money. And nobody cares.

Sonja: Do you think society's attitude has changed towards gays?

Victor: It's hard to say. These days people are kind of self absorbed. How do you survive? How do you feed the family? Gays are the least of their problems. When there wasn't any information about us in Russia, it was the same. Not long ago, in 1995, I dated a man who believed that gay men lost their teeth because they put a penis in their mouths. Do you see the level of information we have? Those Russian gay papers are just complete rags!

Sonja: Have there been any men from ethnic minorities in your circle?

Victor: From the other republics? Yes, I often went to Tashkent in those days, either for work or vacation. It only cost forty-nine rubles. For me that was very inexpensive. I had an Uzbek lover, and I went to see him once a month in Tashkent. I went to Vilnius often, even after I broke up with the guy I was with for three years. I have a lot of friends left in Lithuania, and I never heard, saw or felt any political problems there. Now they say the Lithuanians don't like Russians. Maybe they don't, but gays are everywhere—we have no borders. I traveled to Vilnius, Tashkent [Uzbekistan], and Dushanbe [Tajikistan]. I went all around the entire Soviet Union, and I socialized with gays. There was never anything like: You are Uzbek! Or, you are Russian! Or, you are Jewish! I knew that a gay person could find help anywhere. We'd get together, go out, have fun, recognize all the holidays. We spoke Russian. Everything was great!

Sonja: Why isn't it like that now?

Victor: I think among gays, everything has stayed the same. Although not long ago a friend from Tashkent arrived and said everything was different. The places where gays came together were off limits for Russians. "If you're Russian, go somewhere else." I heard the same about Lithuania. But, from my experience, I have difficulty believing this. I know that gays are the same everywhere, whether you are white or black, Uzbek or Jewish. You have to make friends. If we don't help each other, who will?

Sonja: Do you have any dreams or plans for the future?

Victor: I have dreams like everyone else in Russia. Make money, go somewhere on vacation. At home I don't really need anything. I have an apartment and I have what I need. The important things are work, money, vacation. And of course, I would like to connect with gays outside the country. Learn about how they live. Everything we know is hearsay. Now, of course, the TV has started showing things more often without a lot of negativity, some photos, for example, about gay festivals, people who went there saying things about it. People would go there and stay with a gay couple, they'd hang out and come back and tell us all about it. That's our information.

Sonja: Do you have a long-term partner now?

Victor: Yes, actually I was raised that way. I can love one person or no one. I think Dima is like that too. If he loves someone, it's one person he loves. Of course, if you see an interesting young face, and you sense he is not indifferent to you, all kinds of feelings and desires come up. But right away you think, it's just in the moment. You have someone waiting for you at home. What about him? The town is pretty small, no matter how discreet you might be, everything would be known. So you try to hold yourself together. You have to choose—either to be in a couple or have orgies. It's hard for gays to love only one person. We have learned that the more often you change partners the better. In our times it's difficult to find a person with whom you can be in a normal relationship. One of my friends, about my age, brought a younger guy to live with him. He lived with him about half the year. Then he got everything he wanted out of the apartment and took off.

I am happy with Dima. I think we are very good for each other. He has kind of a low-key personality and so he needs someone to direct him but not inhibit him as a person. I hear him sometimes using my words in group situations, explaining my own thoughts. He absorbs the good stuff and weeds out the bad. Of course, this is flattering. I have helped him a lot. We got together when he was left completely alone. It was terrible. He's not good at casual relations. Since I was robbed, we have accumulated a lot of things together. If we ever have to separate, we would have to divide everything in half, but we don't think about that. We hope to be together a long time. I said, Dima, when I get old, you'll wheel me around in a wheelchair. Joking of course. Yes, he said, I'll take you to the hospital, too. So I will hold onto Dima. I'd love to spend the rest of my life with him, not two or three years and then break up and look for someone else. It's really not hard to find someone. Now there are a lot without apartments and without any money. But I don't want that.

Gossips say he's a taker—you are always thinking of him, doing everything for him; you have your own place, of course, it's good for him. But I say: I'm not fifteen years old and I wouldn't fall in love impulsively without understanding that every person looks out for what's best for him. I thank God that I came across this person in my life path. He's only twenty-five years old. He could say: here's a forty-five year old guy. I don't have residency yet, I'll hook him and live peacefully behind a stone wall. But he's not like that. We have joint finances. It turns out that now Dima has more money than me. His mother and father are doing well. They send him a million rubles every month or so. We basically live on his money, since I am not working right now. Another guy would have long ago gotten rid of me. He didn't do that and I respect him for that.

Sonja: How do you spend your days?

Victor: We share and divide all of our duties. Of course, there are arguments. Who didn't clean the floor? Why didn't you wash the dishes? I have a difficult personality, probably because of my age. His friends even say to me: you're always on Dima's case. Sometimes I get mad and then think: what did I say that for? I could have kept quiet. It's such a little thing—not washing the dishes—and I made such a big deal out of it. Those are little daily problems. He's already OK. Before, he would frown, but now he doesn't pay any attention.

Sonja: Do you want to add anything?

Victor: What can I add? Life is wonderful. Everyone has his own fate. I want to say I am happy with my own life. That's not bravado, it's just true. From this conversation with me, you can see I am not a person of excess. I haven't been in jail and I haven't been really oppressed. I have not had a bad life and, please God, let that continue. But the little things—robberies, and so on—those are minutiae. They give some kind of stimulus to life. You lose one thing and you get another, maybe something even better. I hope that my life with Dima will go on as much as possible. That would be best for him and for me. Of course, it would be great if someone took notice of us in the West, not just spoke about or wrote about us, but if someone could advise us on how to organize ourselves, help with contacts, exchange of information. The rest, we'll do ourselves.

Marina

Interviewed in 1992
Translated by Sonja Franeta

On May 20, 1992, twenty-two year old Marina came to meet me with her friend, Sasha, in tow. Our mutual friends had to persuade Marina over time to let me interview her; nevertheless, despite her reluctance, Marina seemed interested in meeting me. I wanted to interview her when I learned she had passed as a man for three years in order to live with her girlfriend; they even got married as a heterosexual couple. During our interview, she was hesitant to reveal very much about her relationship or any details about their intimate life. Almost a year since their relationship ended, it was still a painful subject for her.

About 5'6" with disheveled mid-length blonde hair and large light blue eyes, Marina was shy and occasionally broke into a dazzling smile. She appeared at the door of our meeting place with a cap on and the bill turned backwards, a motorcycle emblem on it. She wore a T-shirt with the words "Olympia" and blue jeans. She owned a motorcycle.

Marina, an only child, lived on the outskirts of Krasnoyarsk with her parents. Her father was a factory worker and her mother a steward in another factory. Marina did not have a job at the time of the interview but she loved photography.

Irina was her first relationship. They had met in a park in Krasnoyarsk.

Marina: We lived together like a man and a woman for the world, but for us it was something completely different. She was probably bisexual but we loved each other very much. I miss her so much.

I tried to find another girlfriend but I couldn't. What once happen cannot be repeated. I don't want anything else, so it's better to just be alone. Maybe sometime I'll find a girlfriend but not now.

She fell silent and looked sad. I changed the subject and asked what she thought about Asya, Lena, and Olga, the first open lesbian activists in Siberia and our mutual friends. Marina met them by writing a letter to an address they had provided in a newspaper interview.

Marina: I really like what they are doing; it's just great they have brought us all together. We didn't know each other at all before this. Now we have the possibility to be open with each other at least. Everything they are doing is wonderful.

Marina's friend, Sasha, is twenty years old. Her hair is dyed blonde, long and neatly clasped in the back. She wore a beautiful blouse with colorful swirls and light blue jeans. Her eyes are brown and, unlike Marina who looked down most of the time, Sasha watched me intently during the interview. I asked when they each had their first sexual experience with a girl. Marina did not seem to want to answer, so I looked at Sasha.

Sasha: When I was fifteen. I had close girlfriends. Then with some of them, there was sex. Everything seemed perfectly fine. I knew I was lesbian because I was always falling in love with my female teachers, my girlfriends, and then with a famous woman singer.

After high school I went to a technical school and there I met some girls and one came to me to spend the night. We had sex and after that the girl fell in love with me. She had boyfriends at the same time; she was probably bisexual. Then she got married and now she doesn't want women at all. The girl felt that what we did was some kind of perversion and I was hurt.

I have a girlfriend now, her name is Lena. We argue a lot. She has a guy. And when I saw the article in *The Siberian Newspaper*, I wrote to those girls [Asya, Lena, and Olga] and asked them to help me find a girlfriend.

At first, I didn't understand why I was in love with my girlfriends, why I was jealous. I didn't think I was a lesbian at first because I thought all lesbians were in prison, that they were fallen women, corrupt women. Therefore I had nothing in common with them.

I tried to bring Marina into the conversation so I asked her if she considered lesbian a negative word.

Marina: No, I don't, but different people think differently. Some people are interested in us, some hate us. I have a heterosexual girlfriend who knows everything about me. She seems to understand, I think. She even asks me what I do about sex and I tell her everything.

I asked Sasha if her mother knew about her lifestyle.

Sasha: Mama was shocked at first and then she calmed down. I do have a separate room where I can be with my girlfriend. And now my parents go away a lot to their country dacha and I am home alone for days at a time. I like to have parties.

I wanted to get Marina to talk more and so I asked her: since she had passed as a man, did she ever want to become a man?

Marina: No, I didn't. In our home, with us, everything was normal. As soon as I went out the door I became a man. While we were under the same roof, everything was good. We related to each very well. It was very hard to play the role of a man. I always feared revealing myself. I worried that I would give myself away. In summer it's hot, people go around in T-shirts; they go swimming. I had to keep my sweatshirt on, so my breasts couldn't be seen. This was extremely hard—to play the role of a man.

We had our own apartment. We rented it for a year. Then we rented another apartment. It was her grandmother's—Irina's. The apartment was available, not big but it was completely separate. Our first apartment was in Krasnoyarsk then we moved to the village where her grandmother lived.

She stopped and looked down. I remarked that it must have been difficult for her and her girlfriend at times.

Marina: It was not easy, but we survived. It was hard in the very beginning [before we got married] neither of our parents knew we were living together. I had to lie to my own mother saying I was living at a girlfriend's, not with my beloved. At the time Irina was finishing technical school in Krasnoyarsk. Her parents knew she was living there. It was hard, yes. Economically, too, because neither her parents nor mine helped us. And we were still young and foolish.

After that we moved to the village, where Irina's parents were living. At first we lived there with her parents; we had our own room. Then we moved to the grandmother's apartment. Then we began to argue. Before that we never argued, never.

It's my fault that we broke up. If I could have been firmer, stronger in my heart, this wouldn't have happened. She... she's a very soft, tender person. She needed a stronger person, someone with determination, someone she could lean on. But I'm just a woman. I couldn't give her what a man could. I don't know, I can't even explain what I mean. But as for me, I didn't lack anything in my relationship with her.

I asked how the man Irina was with currently came into the picture.

Marina: I was in Krasnoyarsk for a whole month looking for a job and while I was gone he turned up. He knew that Irina was by herself. He knew her from before. He came to her to be with her. He believed I was a guy. So when I left he came to her; they made up and started seeing each other.

When I arrived back home I walked into the apartment and immediately knew a man had been there. When Irina came home, we didn't fight or anything; there were no explanations, we even smiled at one another. We left each other quietly, no arguments. We separated as friends, in other words. It was, of course, very difficult for me to accept, but why make a big scene? We never got together again. She lives with him now and I am here completely alone. I don't think she will leave him. I consider myself a lesbian but she does not. She is a heterosexual woman. Before me, she did not have sex, neither with a man nor woman; I was her first sexual experience. It was natural for her to fall in love with me.

Marina said she had to leave and we parted.

On June 4, 1992, I wanted to speak to Marina again, alone if possible. We sat under a tree in a park at the center of Krasnoyarsk. Marina wore a different cap, this time with the bill forward. Marina still seemed shy but made eye contact more than in our first meeting. Sasha came with her again but this time she sat with our friends on a park bench, further off.

Marina seemed shy. She handed me four photos and said these were the only photos she had of her former beloved. One photo especially struck me. It was their wedding day. Marina had on a tuxedo and her hair was short; she was smiling as her girlfriend planted a kiss on her cheek. If I hadn't known Marina, the photo would have seemed to me like a young, heterosexual couple.

She was a bit more relaxed and open with me this time. When I asked her if she would tell me something about her and her girlfriend's sex life, she was a bit taken aback and said that was too intimate a question. So I asked more about their life together and passing as a man.

Marina: The most difficult part about trying to make people think of me as a man was when I was surrounded by men. I had to be careful about using masculine endings in the first person all the time when I spoke about myself. And you know, you have to always drink and smoke and act like them. I helped some guy fix a motorcycle once. Men are not shy, talking about themselves. They said all kinds of things to me, the most personal things. Of course, they didn't know I was a girl. I remember it was hot once and all the guys were taking off their shirts, but I couldn't.

My mother, when she learned about my actions, thought it was awful. She saw my pictures. She thought I was playing a joke. And Irina, it was all her idea, for me to dress as a man, so that we could be together. We were together for three years, never apart.

Anyway we had a wedding for her parents' benefit. There were a hundred people at Irina's place in the village. We couldn't be together otherwise. If we were living as two women, we would never be considered a couple. Her relatives gave us a double bed for our apartment. We were very much in love with each other. Everyone could see that right away.

Then when I left to go see my mother, after not seeing her for a long time, and came back again, I sensed that a man had been there and that Irina had been with him. When she came home that day, we just cried. She told me not to write, call, or come over anymore. Maybe she still misses me but she's with that man now. They can have children and a regular family life. No one will say anything bad about them, and she doesn't have to hide. I think she still loves me; she must be bisexual.

I never wanted to be a man. I think trans people must be very unhappy. But I think in general it's much easier to be a man than a woman.

The thing that has helped me all this time is my photography. It's the only thing I love, it's my lesbian life now. When I have a hard time I stay in my room, I develop pictures or think of a new idea. I'm not always able to develop and print things because of the cost.

I would love to photograph beautiful women and do more photos about our way of life. I thought of some still life photos I could do—two glasses and two women reflected in the glasses, or cassette tapes with triangles on them, or an unmade bed with two pairs of women's underwear flung on it.

I'm frustrated I can't make large prints and show them to everyone. I'm always afraid my mother will see my work. I don't really want my mother to know about my lifestyle. I would be ashamed to look her in the face. She thinks I was just being bad when I went off with Irina and that I did it to be mischievous. She says I've always been that way. Anyway I don't think it was a very good idea for me to live a lie like that and to fool all those people.

After the interview, we went out for with our friends to a cafe in central Krasnoyarsk where young people sit at tables and have ice cream or coffee. Disco music blared in the background. Marina wore her cap backwards and walked slightly hunched over with a butch swagger. Her light blue eyes sparkled as she mumbled, "Those people at that table over there think I'm a guy." She laughed and ate her ice cream, delighted at her little trick.

Lena and Asya

Interviewed in 1992

Translated by Sonja Franeta

A lifelong dream of mine was to travel across Russia on the Trans-Siberian Railroad. My sense of romance, my Slavic heritage, my studies in Russian literature, my left political leanings—all pointed me in that direction. I yearned to cross one of the most enigmatic countries in the world and experience its expanse firsthand.

In the summer of 1991, I came back home to San Francisco from the Lesbian and Gay Symposium and Film Festival in Moscow and St. Petersburg, with fond memories and many contacts to return to Russia for another visit.

The next spring I decided to travel through Russia on the Trans-Siberian Railway. Before I left San Francisco, I called my Novosibirsk acquaintances, Asya and Lena, whom I had met the summer before at the symposium. I had decided to fly to Khabarovsk and start on the eastern end of enormous Russia, making a stop in Novosibirsk, then continuing on to Moscow. The American independent spirit was not something the Russians were familiar with, so "the girls" insisted on meeting me in Khabarovsk to travel with me to Novosibirsk.

The Trans-Siberian Railroad is the longest continuous track in the world. Our starting point, Khabarovsk, built on the banks of the Amur River, is more than a century old. This eastern Siberian city is the main air junction for Russia's Far East. From Khabarovsk, one can go south to Nakhodka and Vladivostok or west to Lake Baikal, Novosibirsk, or Moscow by train. After Tsar Alexander the III authorized the construction in 1886, it took thirty years to build the railway. In 1916, the year before the October Revolution, it became possible to cross the entire two continents from the English Channel to the Pacific Ocean by train.

Asya and Lena were both in their early twenties, a very attractive couple. Asya was tall with dark short hair and beautiful dark serious eyes, while Lena had curly blonde hair and a playful twinkle in her hazel eyes. As soon as the train quit lurching forward and found its rhythm, Lena set to work arranging our little kupe. She found a rag, wet it, and cleaned all the areas we would be contacting—the vinyl headrests above our berths, the table, the doorknobs. "This train is a lot cleaner than the one we took to get here," she said, shaking her head. We struggled to set my luggage under the bunks after I took out the things I would need—my book, toiletries, a sweater, some snacks.

The conductor (provodnitsa), a large woman in a navy blue uniform, with dyed dark red hair and thick eyebrows, suddenly appeared at our doorway with a bored look on her face, holding a pile of clean linens and muttering something. Lena paid her and then began making up our bunks as if she were at work at the hospital. She was a nurse by profession.

To get out of Lena's way Asya and I stood in the corridor and talked. Asya had a certain confident elegance about her. She had recently left a clerical job at the conservatory of music, where her mother was a piano teacher. Asya spoke English and wanted to learn more so we practiced occasionally on the trip.

Lena pointed us to the other end of the car. Tea was supposedly available but the provodnik (male) or provodnitsa (female) would decide when. The massive samovar in each car was heated by coal and had to be tended by each car's conductor—something she or he didn't always feel like doing. Asya and I went to get the tea water in the three metal cups they had brought with them for the trip.

In our kupe I took naps, lulled by the swaying train and the smell of clean sheets. It was the best way to get over jet lag. There was something very comforting about sleeping whenever you wanted to. The girls pored over the magazines—**Deneuve, the Advocate, Outlook**. Like children with new toys, they shared my Walkman. Occasionally one got impatient and snatched it away from the other, who of course resisted. At such times their youthfulness really showed.

The train made twenty-four stops from Khabarovsk to Novosibirsk. The total distance from Khabarovsk to Moscow is 8,500 km. and the total travel time on the train is seven days and six nights. Even though the scenery was so similar—flat steppes, taiga, tufts of forest punctuated by little settlements of wooden houses with lace-like shutters—I never felt bored. A few people worked in the fields, occasionally a truck drove along the road beside the train tracks, but there were no cars, only tractors or trucks. The steppes were bare, as I had imagined them.

In our homey little kupe, Asya called Lena "koshka" which means cat, and Lena called Asya "zayets" which means rabbit. Often they used these endearments in front of other train travelers. Whenever I remarked on their public affection, they laughed. "Oh, we're sisters. Amazons." Their romance made them glow. Their slurpy kisses echoed from the upper berth. We talked into the night as though we were at camp, Asya's dimples deepening as she laughed, and Lena's head lifting up from Asya's lap to say something.

I asked each of them to tell me when they first felt they were lesbians. Lena was eager to begin, her gray eyes wide open, hands gesturing with abandon. I turned on my tape recorder and began my first real interviews in Russia.

Lena: At college, I became attracted to a girl named Olga. I had a serious crush on her. She wasn't the first girl I felt this way about. I would call her. She thought it was all some kind of joke. I started kissing her, hugging her. By the way, at that time I didn't really know that I was a lesbian. I had heard of such people, but I thought very, very few of them existed and that they were strange. Sometimes friends would say something bad about them. I would agree with these statements, but inside I wanted desperately to meet some of these lesbians. Where were they? How could I meet them?

I was conditioned to dislike and feel disgust toward them. I always said: "Yes, they're awful." But, actually, I myself really wanted to find some of them. How could I get to know them? I wondered.

One day a girlfriend of mine came up to me and said: "I was in the cafe today and there were some gay men there."

I said, "Really? What were they doing?"

"Sitting around a table calling each other Masha and Natasha and other girls' names."

"Oh how awful," I said. "How gross! Foo! Disgusting!" At the same time I was thinking—how I'd love to see them myself!

There was something about them that reflected me, my own outlook. All the same, while I was in school I tried to find myself a boyfriend, because all my friends were dating guys. They were always talking about them with each other, and I didn't want to be different. I wanted to think that I, too, was normal and OK. I, too, wanted to have a boyfriend. I even wanted to marry Olga's brother—to be closer to her. Now, I think what a mistake it would have been, if I had done that.

After school I worked as a nurse in Erfurt, East Germany, in an army hospital. I was glad I went there because it was hard at home. After my brother's death, my parents began divorce proceedings, and this affected me, all their difficulties. I was glad I left home, and that I left Olga. School was over and we had started working. It was hard without her. I couldn't get used to the fact that I would be living another way. I continued to feel attracted to the girls at our hospital.

In Germany I met Tanya. She was about thirty-one, a lot older than me. I don't know what got me about her. She wasn't very pretty, kind of ordinary, but something drew me to her. Again I couldn't believe that I had fallen in love with her. By then I already knew that I was more interested in women, and that I loved being with them.

Tanya was very good to me. She always invited me on walks; she liked to talk with me. But I never was open with her about my attraction to her. I was afraid. That's why we had these heterosexual kind of discussions about men and other things. I just tried to keep up the conversation. Also, I felt attracted to our supervisor, who was about twenty-nine. Tanya and my supervisor, Lena, were very different. While Tanya was slender, Lena was a large woman. I also really liked her.

We lived in a group house and I was always very open and friendly. I would kiss and hug the women in a friendly way. Once I even stroked Lena's breast. It was kind of an accident. She was upset with me for a long time; I myself didn't really know why I did that. This is how it happened: we would all get together, the women and the guys. It was October, the celebration of the reunification of Germany. Russians have this custom—when you get together you have to have drinks. So we drank a little. There was another woman who lived there and who I liked. She was a certain type of person, at least I was sure she had "that" quality. She had a lesbian way about her. Of course, she probably was a lesbian. After everyone left the room and we were alone, she drew me toward her and next thing, she was all over me. We fell on the bed and she continued to kiss me. I got so scared that after a while I ran to my room, thinking, what was all that about, how did that happen? My head was all mixed up, and the next day I was so worried that she would tell someone what happened that night. She was from Belorussia, kind of naive. She was a blabbermouth and said anything that came to her head. That's why I was on edge. She came walking into the room where everyone, all the ones we had partied with, were sitting, and I couldn't believe what she said! "Lenka, remember how we were kissing yesterday?"

I started feeling sick and thought, "Why is she saying this in front of everyone? You don't say things like this."

Sonja: Did anything happen between you two?

Lena: It was all just superficial. After this, I saw a film about two lesbians, the first film about that I ever came across. I thank God that it was a good film. I was twenty or twenty-one. Yes, twenty-one, or

143

twenty-two. I don't remember the name of the film. I think it was called **Emmanuelle**, the series. They showed two women, lesbians, and how one was exposed by her father and then sent to a convent. They showed how they made love; it was all very beautiful. Fantastic film!

When Lena started speaking about how wonderful it was to see **Emmanuelle**, a lesbian film, I remembered my own feelings watching the same film. I was married then, to my husband. How amazing that she and I at different times, at different ages, and in different countries experienced similar feelings and had similar paths to coming out!

Sonja: What did you feel when you met Asya? (I asked Lena, as Asya left the kupe.) Lena: Can you believe the twenty-third of March was supposed be my wedding day, but it was actually the day I met Asya! It turned out to be such an incredibly happy day.

What did I feel? I can't even begin to describe it! I was like a bird! I didn't walk, I flew! I couldn't believe what was happening, yet I felt like I was doing something I've wanted to do all my life. At first I couldn't imagine how I could go to bed with a woman. What would I do? How was this possible? I didn't know anything about sex, making love. Before, I thought that there was only love, that you could just love a woman and that's it. There was no bed. But then when I got it, that all of this was real and it mattered, that there was a bed, that these relationships were possible, and that for me this was...well, I got scared, because really I knew it was somehow forbidden. That's why when I met lesbians, I didn't like them. That was before Asya.

In Novosibirsk, I never had sex with women but I went to Barnaul and met some local women. One of them...well, I wasn't really attracted to her, but she was better than the others. It was nice to hang out with her. They called each other male names and spoke to each other using the male gender. It was as if they were playing the roles of men. I didn't understand that then. When we went to bed (before that we had been kissing, getting excited and I really wanted her), actually when we went to bed I realized I didn't want her because I didn't love her. I didn't like it because I felt like I was around a man, but instead of a man it was a woman. She was doing something and I was thinking: what do I need this for? Not the kind of sex we had. I didn't like it and when I woke up the next morning, I thought, no, I don't want this, it's not me, I don't need this. But at the same time I was thinking, I mean, I really hoped that I would meet the woman for me.

Then I met Asya. And when that other woman from Barnaul called me again, I had to tell her I finally met the woman I wanted. I hadn't promised that woman anything anyway, yet she was very upset, of course. She came to Novosibirsk after that but I didn't see her—she just called me.

I told Asya about this. When Asya first came to spend the night, I was afraid of what would happen. I even said to her, "Asya, maybe I should make up a separate bed for you!" And she said, "Oh come on, let's be together." I was afraid of her and she of me. When we went to bed I realized she was completely inexperienced with sex, and I had to teach her things over time.

I realised all this was already part of me, within me. All my life it was as if I had lived in a shell and walked under some kind of cover. Everything that happened after this was as if my intuition, my nature, my love was leading me there. I have now been with Asya over a year. I love her, she loves me and I think our relationship will be very long. What surprises me is that at the same time that I love her immensely and deeply, this doesn't stop me from being interested in, getting excited about, and even wanting other women. I don't think there's anything wrong with it. I think it even helps one in life.

There was no law against lesbian sex in Soviet Russia, but it was forbidden, as Lena said. I felt I had to explain there was much homophobia in the United States, too. In Russia, I had heard stories of women being institutionalized in psychiatric hospitals and being urged by psychiatrists to either change their sex or to force themselves to go out with men.

I told Asya and Lena that the U.S. was not the mythic land of freedom they thought it was. Homophobia also exists there. I had a friend who suffered electroshock treatments in her youth to "correct" her lesbian inclinations. Gay bashing occurred in the gay capital of San Francisco. They listened to me but they didn't seem to believe me.

Asya was not as willing as Lena to talk. Perhaps it was just difficult for her to open up. She thought deeply but she was also quite moody. I had to catch her when the time was right on our four-day journey to Novosibirsk. I liked watching her shop for food at the train stations. She seemed to enjoy it. I usually went with her out of curiosity but she was quite fast. I sometimes lost her in the crowds.

"When did you first identify as a lesbian?" I ventured, as the train started off, hoping she would at last want to talk. Staring out the window, she spoke softly in her sexy, deep voice.

Asya: I think I knew when I was twenty, no, twenty-one. But I have thought about it since I was sixteen, in the sense that I thought there was something different about me. I thought there was something special, really, but it didn't bother me. It amused me that I liked women and I thought there was nothing wrong with that and it was just one of my interests. I have always related very easily to my inclinations and to those of others. I was not judgmental if someone did not have the same interests as me and everyone else.

When I found out about lesbians, I was about eighteen. I found out that there were such women. I never thought of them as bad, but I thought that they were just as good as me.

I even identified myself as such at that time. But you know, it wasn't that serious. I could never say: this is who you are and you'll always be that way. No, very quietly I took on that name—lesbian. Then later when I was twenty-one, I wrote a letter to an activist in Barnaul and said I was a lesbian and that I was not with anyone but I wanted to find a girlfriend. I was twenty-one then. I said it all very simply and easily.

Sonja: Did you have any experience with girlfriends in your childhood?

Asya: No, only in my early childhood, not very serious, when we were all exploring our bodies. It was interesting to see what others were like. Were they the same as you or something different? Ever since childhood I knew that I really liked girls, that sometimes I would find myself thinking about one all day and all night, and then I'd go to school and look at her over and over and think about her even more.

Sonja: Did you have girlfriends you were interested in?

Asya: Yes, but the ones I really wanted were not my girlfriends—either someone I barely knew or didn't know at all. For example, once I was simultaneously interested both in a classmate of mine and in some singer or violinist where my mother worked. At one time I liked women of my age and older.

I wanted a woman, physically, ever since the age of eighteen. I knew I wanted a woman and not a man. But up until the age of twenty, I had no experience. Nothing beyond a little hug or sleeping in the same bed. There was no other experience, nothing romantic, just friendship. I never acted on my feelings. I never allowed myself to. I don't know why, why I limited myself. I could never admit what I felt for a girl, I could not understand what was going on. And really, these feelings were so long ago.

I just felt that there would finally come a time when I would know what to say or do and not be afraid, and it would be a person like me, a person who would understand everything. My first experience was actually with this person, a person who understood me, and that person is Lena. It was also the first time for her. Actually Lena is my first and only experience with a woman.

Sonja: And what did you feel?

Asya: Oyy...Sonja, the feelings were so amazing. I tried to write them down. It was as if wings grew out of my shoulders. It was truly a first love. The truest true love. Although I did have another first love, it was another kind. This was the most wonderful thing that ever happened to me, my life. That's why I don't ever want to lose Lena.

I never felt any kind of confusion or agitation, maybe just a little, the first few hours we all got together at Benjamin's place. Alexey, Olga, Lena and another girl was there, too. When I saw how Benjamin and Alexey were hugging and kissing each other, I got a little foggy or something. I had to get used to it. But I liked it. I really did. Because it was very dear and they are sweet guys, so warm and friendly.

When I finally got used to the idea that I was among my own people, that I could speak freely and be completely open, I simply did what I wanted to do—I took Lena's leg and stroked it.

We were sitting at a table and she had on a short black skirt and panty hose. At first we did not really pay much attention to each other. I thought she wasn't attracted to me and she thought I was not attracted to her so we were kind of shy around each other. I sat next to her. I couldn't eat or drink, I couldn't do anything. Nothing happened. I only wanted Lena; I wanted to be with her. All the while I was getting up to smoke, smoke, smoke. Finally I got brave and sat down right next to her. I shoved my hand under the table so no one would see and then I noticed her hand coming towards mine. We just grabbed each other's hands and I knew then that I had nothing to fear with Lena. I could tell her everything and do everything I wanted.

The compartment door suddenly clicked and slid open. Lena looked at us sleepily saying she was hungry. "I'll get the tea ready right away, kotyonok." Asya brushed Lena's permed hair away from her face, then kissed her on the lips.

Central Asian soldiers traveled with us in the train. They seemed friendly and polite. However, the girls were making all kinds of prejudicial remarks about them. "The Azerbaijanis are so crafty. And Russians are so innocent and passive and that's why they get hoodwinked by them," said Asya. It was not only that the Azerbaijanis were a darker race, but that they were merchants, as I understood, and Russians resented this.

"And the Tatars can wrap the Russians around their little fingers. Don't I have you wrapped around my finger, zayets?" said Lena leaning close to Asya. "You're not a Tatar, you're a Russian" said Asya, pushing her away. Pure Russians were nowhere to be found, especially in Siberia. Our Lena was actually a Tatar [the third largest nationality in Russia after Russian and Ukrainian].

We had been talking about Asya's experience with men and the guy she was with before Lena. He was Central Asian.

Sonja: Did you ever have any relationships with men?

Asya: Yes, when I was eighteen, all of a sudden I fell for a guy. And he fell in love with me too. We had a very open and close relationship which lasted a couple of years, right before I turned twenty. It was my first love that I really wanted and longed for. When I was sixteen and all my friends were falling in love, I started thinking why can't I fall in love and why doesn't anyone fall in love with me? Then when I turned eighteen, I met a young man and we fell in love with each other. I don't regret anything about it. It wasn't a distraction or a whim—it was really a first love. I felt a lot and agonized, for everything was not the same as before I was eighteen.

I tried very hard, it seemed. I had to, I had to. Finally I fell in love with a man. I had a lot of friends but there was no one else I could fall in love with. They were all good, wonderful, they even asked me out. There was one friend from childhood who still follows me around. As soon as I'd come back home from somewhere, he was there, "Asya, did you think it over?" I didn't like men anymore, I just didn't like them at all. Not because I think they are jerks. I just don't like them. They are not interesting to me.

The person I loved was just a person. I loved him like a person. Here's something interesting: I never wanted sex with him, never! I loved his soul only because he related well to me, because he was cheerful, kind and smart, but I never wanted sex with him. I loved him but I wanted sex with women.

He was from Central Asia, from Tashkent. After I met him, my mother and I started having major arguments. She is... well, you already know about my mother. She doesn't like Armenians, Uzbeks, Jews, or Georgians. She only likes Russians. She doesn't like homosexuals, lesbians, drug addicts, prostitutes, only Russians and that's all, and only the good ones. That's that. Therefore it was really awful for her that I was with him.

Sonja: She didn't like your choice?

Asya: No, she never liked my choices. She only liked the friends I had since my childhood, with whom I grew up. She considered them good. But anyone I ever had feelings for, as a grownup, she rejected. She had certain limited stereotypes—the good ones are only those who have degrees, like herself. Before, it was very prestigious to receive a higher degree. But I haven't been able to finish one myself. So a person with a higher degree is the only person you can fully relate to. She was constantly reproaching me: "All your friends work who knows where, they don't want an education." Then about Lena; "Look at your nurse." My nurse? What did she mean, my nurse? She knew.

Sonja: A nurse? Did she mean she was a different class?

Asya: She was purposely insulting her by calling her a nurse. And she was always making remarks about her nationality. She called her, "Your Tatar."

I answered her: "Well, of course she's mine." What else could I say? My mother only wanted me to hang out with people who achieved some sort of intellectual level. She never approved of my friends.

We chugged by the endless shore of Lake Baikal, still somewhat covered by ice at the edges. It was one of the most incredible sights I saw during my travels in Russia. Huge chunks of ice were breaking up along its shores; people stood at its edges with fishing poles. Our train went alongside it for two hours, sometimes as close as several yards away from the water. Lake Baikal is the world's deepest (1.6 kilometers) and oldest lake (twenty-five million years or more). Over 365 rivers flow into it and only one river, the Angara, flows out of it. People in our car lined the windows reverently.

A woman in the corridor who had been looking at Lena and Asya kissing and hugging, asked them if they were sisters. "We are all sisters," Asya laughed, embracing both Lena and me, "Amazon sisters!"

We went to sleep for the last leg of our journey. The train seemed to be making up for lost time, speeding along the tracks furiously, bouncing and rocking us around. I felt cold. The provodnitsa must have decided not to turn on the heat.

When I woke up, Lena was climbing down from the upper berth with Asya, to get into her own bed across from me. Lena noticed me open my eyes and we both smiled. She bent over and kissed me on the forehead. I felt comforted and happy; they had taken such good care of me and of each other. I did not know that this would be the start of a long relationship I would have with Siberia—or that Asya and Lena would break up in less than a year.

Sonja Franeta is a writer, translator, and educator, living in Florida with her spouse, Sue, and their two cats. She worked in Moscow and Novosibirsk and traveled throughout Russia, Siberia, and the Ukraine. The idea of doing a book of LGBT interviews germinated while she served as a delegate to the first Russian Lesbian and Gay Symposium and Film Festival in July of 1991. **Розовые Фламинго** [Pink Flamingos], first published in 2004 in Russian, is translated into English in this volume. Sonja's writing has appeared in journals and anthologies in the U.S., in the Moscow lesbian journal **Ostrov** [Island] and in other foreign publications. **My Pink Road to Russia**, her 2015 book of stories, essays, and memoirs in English was inspired by her work in Russia. She holds Master's Degrees in Russian literature from New York University and in Comparative Literature from the University of California at Berkeley.

www.ingramcontent.com/pod-product-compliance
Lightning Source LLC
Chambersburg PA
CBHW060459280326
41933CB00014B/2798